TEN SECRETS FOR A
SUCCESSFUL FAMILY

TEN SECRETS FOR A SUCCESSFUL FAMILY

Adrian Rogers

CROSSWAY BOOKS • WHEATON, ILLINOIS
A DIVISION OF GOOD NEWS PUBLISHERS

Ten Secrets for a Successful Family

Copyright © 1996 by Adrian Rogers

Published by Crossway Books
a division of Good News Publishers
1300 Crescent Street
Wheaton, Illinois 60187

All rights reserved. No part of this publication may be reproduced, stored in a retrieval system or transmitted in any form by any means, electronic, mechanical, photocopy, recording or otherwise, without the prior permission of the publisher, except as provided by USA copyright law.

Cover design/illustration: Cindy Kiple

First printing, 1996

First trade paperback edition, 1998

Printed in the United States of America

Unless otherwise indicated, Bible quotations are taken from the King James Version

Library of Congress Cataloging-in-Publication Data
Rogers, Adrian.
 Ten secrets for a successful family : a perfect ten for homes that win / Adrian Rogers.
     p.   cm.
 Includes bibliographical references.
 ISBN 0-58134-033-8
 1. Family—Religious life.   2. Child rearing—Religious aspects—
Christianity.   3. Ten commandments.   I. Title.
BV4526.2.R64   1996
248.4—dc20   95-52024

11	10	09	08	07	06	05	04	03	02	01	00	99	98
20	19	18	17	16	15	14	13	12	11	10	9 8 7 6 5 4 3 2 1		

This work is gratefully dedicated to my family,
the strong heartbeat of my life:

JOYCE
*childhood sweetheart, wife, partner, love,
friend, and godly mother*

STEVE
*firstborn son, creative musician,
man of God, faithful husband, and father*

GAYLE
*firstborn daughter, counselor, leader,
godly wife, and mother*

PHILIP
*our son in heaven
we can hardly wait to see you*

DAVID
*loyal son, missionary, theologian,
bold witness, loving husband and father*

JANICE
*baby daughter, creative teacher,
loving wife and mother*

MY GRANDCHILDREN
they are the greatest!

*"Praise ye the Lord. Blessed is the man that feareth
the LORD,* that delighteth greatly in his commandments.
His seed shall be mighty upon earth: the generation
of the upright shall be blessed."

—Psalm 112:1-2

CONTENTS

ACKNOWLEDGMENTS

I want to thank my coworkers and friends whose encouragement and support helped to bring this book into being: the staff at Love Worth Finding Ministries; Linda Glance, my faithful secretary who spent many hours typing portions of this material; President Lane Dennis, Vice President Leonard Goss, Managing Editor Ted Griffin, and all the great folks at Crossway Books; and my editor and friend, Philip Rawley.

INTRODUCTION

I have one great burning ambition in my life apart from maintaining my personal devotional love for the Lord Jesus Christ.

That ambition, that desire, that objective is that my family—my wife, children, and grandchildren—know and love the Lord Jesus Christ and that they love one another. My life's verse, Psalm 112:1–2, as quoted in the dedication of this book, reflects the prayer and desire of my heart. Closely related to that is 3 John 4—"I have no greater joy than to hear that my children walk in truth."

I want my family to be a successful family. I want my home to be a home that wins. I don't measure success by the "B's"—brains, bucks, beauty, brawn, and bigness. Sometimes these can be "killer B's."

My heart's desire is that my family love God and love one another; and that while they are doing it, they will be an example to bring this lost world to Jesus Christ.

But today all of the artillery of hell seems to be aimed at the nuclear family—humanism, relativism, materialism, hedonism. This book is written to give the family some weapons for the warfare. The chief weapon in our arsenal is truth that brings a fixed standard for right and wrong, and that truth is encapsulated in the Ten Commandments.

I am afraid that our generation has thought the Ten Commandments are more or less like corn flakes—familiar, old, and not very exciting. But I want to encourage you to "taste them again for the first time."

I have sometimes called the Ten Commandments "a perfect ten for homes that win." They are just that. These Commandments are not accidental or incidental but fundamental.

I am told that a salesman was driving through the country trying to get to a certain city. He came to a fork in the road and stopped to question a farmer. "Does it make any difference which of these roads I take?" The farmer answered, "Not to me it doesn't."

I am afraid that many of America's politicians, preachers, and teachers feel the same way. I can tell you, however, that when it comes to righteousness and truth, it makes a great deal of difference which road we take.

The Ten Commandments were given primarily to the home, and they were to be taught by fathers to their children and grandchildren, as we will see later in this book.

These Commandments are rock-ribbed and ironclad, but they are not cold, rigid restrictions. Properly understood, they are the liberating laws of life.

Jesus did not come to abolish the law but to fulfill it. When we know Him in repentance and faith, the righteousness of the law is fulfilled in us (Romans 8:4).

Don't be afraid of God's holy law. Don't let legalism make the law a burden, and don't allow license to make the law an irrelevancy.

In legalism, the law is my master.

In license, the law is my enemy.

In liberty, the law is my friend.

I send this work from my hand to your heart with a prayer and with confidence. My confidence is based on two things:

The Ten Commandments are part of the infallible, inerrant Word of God. I have great confidence there.

Also, at this stage of life I have personal experience that generates confidence. I am reminded of the preacher who said that when he was young he had four sermons on child-rearing and no children. He confessed that later he had four children and no sermons.

I have four children and plenty of experience. I have been a pastor for four decades. I have pastored small churches with a few dozen members, and my present congregation numbers over 25,000.

But the real experience I cherish is that of a happy husband who married his childhood sweetheart and is passionately in love with her. I have four godly and happily married children and seven incredible grandchildren.

Bragging? Nope! Just praising God for His goodness.

I trust that the Ten Commandments will be the basis of godliness in your home. My prayer is that your home will discover God's "perfect ten," and that as a result it will be a little colony of heaven down here on earth.

1

IT TAKES GOD TO
MAKE A HOME

The life of the nation is the life of the family written large.

—*Plato*

Something terrible is happening in America. We are losing out spiritually in our homes, and the results of our loss are being felt in every corner of society.

Let me give you two illustrations to help set the stage for what I want to share with you in this book. Not too long ago the cover of *Newsweek* magazine was emblazoned with the word *Shame*. Under it was the question, "How do we bring back a sense of right and wrong?" That's quite a topic for the secular press to be tackling, wouldn't you agree?

The article says, "Shame—that's something they have over in Japan, isn't it? Our country's about shame*less*ness. Here we have TV shows where people tell the world about bestiality inside their bedroom—and the world yawns."[1] In an accompanying sidebar article, Kenneth Woodward writes:

> Ninety percent of Americans say they believe in God. Yet the urgent sense of personal sin has all but disappeared in the current upbeat style in American religion. . . . In earlier eras, ministers regularly exhorted congregations to humbly "confess our

sins." But the aging baby boomers who are rushing back to church do not want to hear sermons that might rattle their self-esteem. And many clergy, who are competing in a buyer's market feel they cannot afford to alienate.[2]

Now, if we are losing the battle for basic decency and subsequently for our homes, then somebody better be rattling our self-esteem! The preacher's job is not to fill the auditorium, but to fill the pulpit.

Whether people want to hear the truth or not, we've got to stop marketing religion and pandering to people's desires. Our nation's moral and spiritual crisis is much too deep-rooted to allow for superficial fixes. Even nonreligious people in America are beginning to realize that we are facing disintegration as a society. This is a problem of fundamental values.

No wonder our young people are so confused. I feel sorry for today's youth, which brings me to my second illustration. I saw a young man in an airport recently. I suppose he was about eighteen years of age. He had an earring in one ear, a lot of facial hair, and he was wearing a T-shirt.

I took out my pen and wrote down what it said on the back of that shirt. Here it is: "I am not scared. I am not afraid. I am an animal. I will eat you alive if I have to. NO FEAR." This was the first shirt of that kind I had seen. Now there is a whole line of clothing with that basic theme.

This young man wanted the world to know he was not afraid. But you know something? I think he was very much afraid.

We used to have a cat. When a dog would come around, our cat would puff up real big. But the reason he puffed up was because he was afraid of that dog. This generation may talk big, but it experiences a great deal of fear—and much of it is homemade.

LOSING A GENERATION

So we are raising a generation of youngsters who feel like animals, ready to eat us alive! And why shouldn't they? They've been systematically taught that they *are* animals, that they were not created in the image of God. Instead, they are accidents of nature. That's why that teenager in the airport felt it was important to advertise that he was not afraid— because he was an animal.

With this kind of mind-set, is it any wonder that our children and young people often behave like animals? More than 100,000 of our young people are caged in prisons today. More than a million teenage girls in America will get pregnant this year. And more than ten million minors are infected with sexually transmitted diseases. So much for the animal farm!

It doesn't sound like our homes are very successful, does it? But the thesis and the heart of this book is that we *can* have homes that win—homes that not merely survive, but thrive.

God has a plan to give us successful homes. It is given to us in His Word and is communicated in divine shorthand in the Ten Commandments, His perfect law. If we want to have homes that win, we can rediscover God's will as revealed in His Ten Commandments. That's my primary goal for this book—to give you a strategy and a plan to transport God's perfect plan for the home from the pages of Scripture right into your living room. Obviously, biblical instruction on the home is not confined to the Ten Commandments. But in this book our focus will be primarily on that crucial and foundational section of the Word of God. This is not the totality of God's communication on the subject, but it is a good starting point and is a strategic portion of what God wants to say to us.

Many of our young people today could not recite the Ten Commandments if their lives depended on it, even many who are members of Bible-teaching churches. One reason is that their parents don't know the Commandments either, except for some vague idea of right and wrong. Today kids have computers in their bedrooms, but they're becoming roadkill on the information highway.

There is a war going on in America, a battle for the soul of our nation. The battleground is the home, and *the issue is truth*. Satan has aimed all of the artillery of hell at our homes, and every shell in that artillery is a lie.

Satan's chief weapon is deception. The devil would rather peddle a lie than a barrel of whiskey or a kilo of illegal drugs any day. Satan would rather get you to believe a wrong thing than to do a wrong thing. He is the sinister minister of destruction.

Why? Because a lie is the most dangerous thing on the face of this earth. It is antithetical to God, who is the Truth and whose Word is truth (John 17:17). Satan is a pusher of lies, because the thought is the father of the deed. And if he can get a nation to move away from truth, if the foundation is destroyed, what can the righteous do?

Recent polls indicate that the majority of Americans no longer believe in absolute truth. And here's the frightening thing—some 62 percent of the people who call themselves evangelical Bible believers say there is no such thing as absolute truth. Now you can begin to see why our generation has lost its standards, its moorings, its moral compass. We now have morality by majority, and the result is chaos in society.

I'm weary of hearing about the religious right and the religious left. The issue is not right or left. The issue is right and wrong. Let me say again, the issue is truth.

God has given us His Ten Commandments, His unfailing and perfect plan for life, and we'll never have homes that are victorious and happy without them. They may be "secrets" to the world, but they are God's clear revelation to anyone who will heed them and teach them to their children. That's what I want to help you do in this book.

I realize that to some people the Ten Commandments may fall into the category of black-and-white television—okay for its time, but sort of out of date. But as we begin this study my challenge to you is to hear and heed them afresh.

Preparing the Way

In the chapters that follow we will look at each of the Ten Commandments in detail, and at the end of each chapter I will give you some specific ideas to help you communicate God's truth to your family.

But before we home in on Exodus 20, I want to show you how vital this is and prepare the way by considering what many people believe to be the most important passage in all of the Old Testament—Deuteronomy 6:1-9, which includes the great *Shema* of Israel. Here Moses tells us how we are to observe and teach God's Commandments.

Something hit me like a hammer as I was pondering this passage in the preparation of these studies. It clearly shows how God wants to communicate the Ten Commandments to His people. Are you ready for it? Here it is: from father to son. It's that simple.

The Ten Commandments were not meant to be taught primarily in the public school, the halls of government, or the boardrooms of business.

These places may be well and good, and the truth of God is certainly needed there, but they are not God's ideal plan. The primary setting for the communication of the Ten Commandments is the home. With that in mind, let's consider the teachings and applications of this great text.

The book of Deuteronomy is Moses' farewell address to the people of Israel just before they entered the Promised Land. He was reminding the people of God's dealings with them and was preparing them to live in a way that would please God and guarantee them a future. Moses knew that God's answer to the chaos of pagan society was the family, and he wanted to strengthen and equip Israel's families to stand strong.

To set the context of Deuteronomy 6, we need to back up to chapter 5. In verses 6-21 of that chapter, Moses restated the Ten Commandments as he had received them from the Lord on Mount Sinai. Notice verse 29, where Moses is speaking for God and says:

> Oh that there were such an heart in them, that they would fear me, and keep all my commandments always, that it might be well with them, and *with their children for ever!* (emphasis mine)

Let me tell you, it will not be well with us and with our children if we do not make some radical changes and begin teaching the Ten Commandments in our homes.

Now look at the opening verses of Deuteronomy 6:

> Now these are the commandments, the statutes, and the judgments, which the LORD your God commanded to teach you, that ye might do them in the land whither ye go to possess it: that thou mightest fear the LORD thy God, to keep all his statutes and his commandments, *which I command thee, thou, and thy son, and thy son's son, all the days of thy life; and that thy days may be prolonged.* Hear therefore, O Israel, and observe to do it; that it may be well with thee, and that ye may increase mightily, as the LORD God of thy fathers hath promised thee, in the land that floweth with milk and honey.
> —Verses 1-3, emphasis mine

God says that if you want your home and your nation to last, then take these Commandments and hand them down from father to son.

What a wonderful "winning streak" that would be for our homes—God's Commandments being handed down generation after generation.

We need homes that succeed with God because our kids have lost something. I'm very concerned about the generation growing up today. So many children and young people attend churches filled with squishy theology, where the authority of the Word of God is questioned and the life of the Lord Jesus Christ is not being manifest, where the worship is empty and futile.

It has well been said that in the fifties kids lost their innocence. They seemed to be liberated by music and films and cars and money.

Then after losing their innocence, in the sixties kids lost their authority. During that decade of rebellion, young people challenged every authority—their parents, teachers, religion, government. But nothing replaced those authorities, so the youth were left without anything to believe.

That led to a loss of the ability to love in the seventies and especially in the eighties, the so-called "me-decade." Having lost their ability to love, young people substituted sex for love without knowing the difference.

So in our day, having lost their innocence, authority, and ability to love, our youth have lost their hope. That's why young people in the bloom of life are taking their lives. They have lost any confidence in the future. It breaks my heart to see this happening.

James Madison is called the father of the American Constitution. Here is what he said about our nation: "We have staked the whole future of American civilization, not upon the power of government, far from it. We have staked the future of our politics upon the capacity of each and all of us to govern ourselves, to control ourselves according to the Ten Commandments of God."

Madison said that America had staked everything on the ability of its people to govern themselves and control themselves according to the Ten Commandments. That's an incredible statement! It wasn't a pulpit-pounding preacher who said that. It was the father of the Constitution.

But the Ten Commandments have been all but lost in our homes. And even though I said above that the public schools are not God's primary place for the communication of the Commandments, at least several generations of American schoolchildren were able to read them on the walls of their schools.

But no more! The Ten Commandments have been removed from America's schools. One would think they are a sinister plan for the overthrow of the government and so must be banned from the vulnerable minds of students.

Who are we listening to today? Not to James Madison, but to people like the scientist Carl Sagan, who stands before the TV camera and confidently announces, "The cosmos is all there is."

Well, if this universe is all there is, the idea of a God must be obsolete. And if God is obsolete, His Commandments must be obsolete—an archaic code for a musty age.

But I want to say that the Ten Commandments are not obsolete. They are *absolute*—absolutely true and absolutely necessary. And America's homes cannot hope to survive apart from the moral foundation they provide. Here is what God says fathers and mothers are to do with His Ten Commandments in the home:

> Hear, O Israel: The LORD our God is one LORD: and thou shalt love the LORD thy God with all thine heart, and with all thy soul, and with all thy might. And these words, which I command thee this day, shall be in thine heart: and thou shalt teach them diligently unto thy children, and shalt talk of them when thou sittest in thine house, and when thou walkest by the way, and when thou liest down, and when thou risest up. And thou shalt bind them for a sign upon thine hand, and they shall be as frontlets between thine eyes. And thou shalt write them upon the posts of thy house, and on thy gates.
>
> —Verses 4-9

EMBRACING GOD'S TRUTH

Here is the great *Shema* (taken from the first word, "Hear")—Israel's confession of faith. As I said earlier, the Jews consider this to be the most important passage in the book of Deuteronomy, if not in the entire Bible. Orthodox Jews would repeat it at least twice a day. They would repeat it in the congregation. God says primarily to fathers but also to mothers, "Teach My commands to your children."

Remember the background here. Moses has restated the Ten

Commandments in Deuteronomy 5, and now God tells the people through Moses to teach these truths to their children.

We complain that the Ten Commandments can no longer be posted in public places. May I meddle a little? How many Christian parents know the Ten Commandments? How many of us have the Ten Commandments posted in our homes or in our minds?

God told Moses, "Tell the people to put these laws upon the doorposts of their houses." And God says to fathers today, "It is your responsibility, not the government's or the school's responsibility, to teach these Commandments to your children." Dad, it's your job. I don't know where we got the idea that teaching God's Word and spiritual truth to children has been assigned to the school or is strictly women's work. The Bible always places the primary responsibility on fathers. Dads, the onus is on us. We cannot punt the ball to our wives or the government or the school. It is up to us to see that the Ten Commandments are handed down to our children.

Psalm 127:4 says, "As arrows are in the hand of a mighty man; so are children of the youth." Fathers are God's mighty warriors to launch their children like arrows straight and true to the bull's-eye. If you have ever tried to bend and string a large bow like those used in archery competitions, you know how hard it is. It's even harder to pull the bow back and fire the arrow if you're not used to it. It takes strength and skill.

A father who wants to shoot straight as a warrior must be strong and skilled. Dads can't fire their "arrows" straight unless they are developing their own spiritual, mental, and emotional strength.

But fathers must also shape and sharpen their twigs into arrows. Children are not born arrows—they are born twigs. We are all twisted by sin from the womb. So the Bible tells parents to raise their sons and daughters in the "nurture and admonition of the Lord" (Ephesians 6:4).

Further, the warrior's aim must be true. He must keep the target in sight. What are your goals for your children? What target do you want them to hit? Are you helping aim them toward God's will for their lives?

Once you sight the target, you need to fire the arrows. Arrows are not meant to be collected. They are to be projected. Our ultimate goal is to release our children spiritually and emotionally, not to try and keep them in the "quiver."

All of that is primarily the responsibility of the father. That's why I am thankful for the renewed attention being focused on fatherhood today. Amazingly, all of the studies and anecdotal evidence being gathered points to what the Bible has taught for centuries. If a husband and father is not the head of the family, the result can only be chaos. The father is God's person to lend stability and character and strength to the home.

Sadly, many dads today are interested in sports and business and sex, but have forgotten their God-given responsibility to teach their sons and daughters about the Word of God, including the Ten Commandments. Our society is being devastated by the growing dilemma of negligent or absent fathers.

"Fatherlessness is the most harmful demographic trend of this generation," says David Blankenhorn, author of a book called *Fatherless America*. He goes on to say that fatherlessness is also "the engine driving our most social problems, from crime to adolescent pregnancy to child sexual abuse to domestic violence against women."[3]

The great problem today is not delinquent kids, but dropout dads and misguided moms who have failed to hand down God's truths from one generation to another. For the most part, a juvenile delinquent is simply a child trying to act like his parents.

To keep from being that kind of parent and that kind of Christian, we need to mine this great passage in Deuteronomy 6 and see what God would have us learn.

The Great Revelation: One Lord

"Hear, O Israel: The LORD our God is one LORD" (Deuteronomy 6:4). Here is the great revelation. There is just one God, one Jehovah, one Lord.

Everybody is going to believe in something or some kind of a god. But we're not just talking about the god of your choice here. Moses says the Lord God of Israel is unique. He is the only God. There is no other.

The Great Response: One Love

How should we respond to such a great revelation? "And thou shalt love the LORD thy God with all thine heart, and with all thy soul, and with all thy might" (verse 5).

The great revelation: one Lord. The great response: one love. And what kind of love? You are to love God with a *sincere* love—"with all thine heart." Jesus spoke of people who "honoreth me with their lips; but their heart is far from me" (Matthew 15:8).

Do you know what your children need to see in your home? They need to see a sincere love for God. They need to see in you a burning, passionate, emotional sincerity when it comes to the things of God. Kids can spot a phony a mile away, and they know whether or not you love God with all your heart. It is the phoniness of parents, by and large, that turns kids off to the things of God.

My four grown children know I'm not perfect. But if you ask them, they will tell you that their dad is not a phony. They know he loves God with a sincere love.

You're also to love God with a *selfless* love—"with all thy soul" (verse 5). Your soul is your self, your being. What is Moses saying? To love God with your whole self, the totality of your being. Your whole self needs to be given to God. There needs to be no area in your life that is off-limits to God.

We could pretty well measure the spiritual love of men or women by looking at two books in their home—their checkbook and their date book—their bank account and their calendar. How you spend your money and your time says a lot about how selfless your love for God is.

Finally, we are commanded to love God with a strong love—"with all thy might." That means every inch, every ounce, every nerve, every sinew of your body. But Moses is not just talking here about physical strength. This includes any kind of strength you may have—emotional strength, financial strength, intellectual strength. You are to use it all in loving God.

The Great Responsibility: One Law

There's a third thing I want you to see in Deuteronomy 6. Because we have the great revelation of the one Lord who demands the great response of love, there is also the great responsibility—one law. One Lord, one love, one law.

Verses 6-7 of this tremendous passage give us our great responsibility:

> And these words, which I command thee this day [not ten sugges-
> tions or voluntary initiatives!], shall be in thine heart: and thou
> shalt teach them diligently unto thy children, and shalt talk of

them when thou sittest in thine house, and when thou walkest by
the way, and when thou liest down, and when thou risest up.

Did you know your home is to be a law school? You're to teach the
law of God. The professors are to be mom and dad, but primarily dad.
We saw earlier in verse 2 that the primary emphasis is upon the father
as the teacher of spiritual truth.

Now if you are from a broken home, or if you are a single parent trying to raise your children alone, I don't want to discourage you. After
each of the next ten chapters in which we will study the Ten
Commandments one at a time in detail, you will find ideas to help you
make up for an absent partner. My desire is to help and undergird. But
I'm saying that something has to be done about our homes.

There are powerful forces trying to shape and mold the mentality of
today's youth. Many of them come home, go to their bedrooms, shut the
door, and turn on a moral sewer called Music Television (MTV).
Anybody who thinks kids aren't affected by what they see has rooms to
rent upstairs. Why would a company pay one million dollars for a thirty-
second commercial during the Super Bowl if what people see doesn't
affect them?

It's time for us to wake up and smell the coffee. Our homes are to be
law schools where God's Commandments are taught. The professors in
this law school are primarily fathers, the students are the children, and
class is already in session!

Teaching God's Ten Great "Secrets"

I want to give you five ways you can teach your children God's plan as
taught in the Ten Commandments. But before I do that, let me encourage you to start training your kids now, wherever you are. You can't
begin too early when it comes to teaching the things of God. So let's
consider five ways to teach the Ten Commandments, drawn from
Deuteronomy 6:6-9.

Teach Them Convincingly

How do you teach the Ten Commandments in your home? Teach them
convincingly. Notice in verse 6 that "these words" are to be in your heart

first. If you don't believe something, if you don't practice it, just hang it up, because you'll never teach it.

Don't send your children to Sunday school or to the local Christian school and think you have done your duty. I tell the people in my church that it's not my responsibility to teach their children. Certainly I have a teaching responsibility as pastor, but my role is to support the teaching in the home, not to substitute for it. God's truth must be in your heart. You can't teach it convincingly to your children unless you're convinced.

Teach Them Consistently

God's Word should be taught consistently or diligently. In verse 7a we read, "Thou shalt teach them diligently unto thy children."

Your teaching needs to be "precept upon precept; line upon line" (Isaiah 28:10). Build truth on top of truth; teach the Word over and over again. Don't say, "Well, I told them that. What's next?" Your children might need to hear that particular truth or exhortation again. Few, if any, of us, learn everything we're supposed to the first time around.

Too many of us start and then quit, then start again and quit again. Be consistent in your teaching. You don't have to do it all in one day. The cumulative effect of "line upon line" teaching—spiritual compound interest—is wonderful.

Teach Them Creatively

You also need to teach God's Word creatively (verse 7). Use every means at your disposal. When our children (now grown) were young, Joyce and I used Bible reading, Bible stories, Bible games, Bible memory, and Christian books and songs to teach them. Praise God for the variety of methods and resources available to us!

The problem in many homes is that we suddenly get on a religion "jag" and say, "You kids are going to learn the Bible. So sit still while I instill." That's not the way God's Word is to be taught.

Charlie Jones, the great motivator, had a boy who was going to be sixteen before long. Charlie told him, "Son, when you get to be sixteen you're going to want a car, and I am going to help you buy a car.

"But before then there are some books I want you to read and give me a report on. I'll select the books. You read the books and write me a report, and for every book you read you'll get ten dollars for your car fund."

Why did Charlie Jones do that? As he told his son, "If you read like a bum, you'll drive like a bum."

That's good. Put some motivation into this thing. You say, "I don't believe in bribing kids." It's not a bribe. It's a reward. A bribe is an inducement to do evil. A reward is incentive for doing good. God rewards, and parents should reward too.

Teach Them Conversationally

The Ten Commandments should be taught conversationally. In verse 7, we're instructed to teach God's Word in the normal course of daily discourse. Later, in verse 20, we read:

> And when thy son asketh thee in time to come, saying, What mean the testimonies, and the statutes, and the judgments, which the LORD our God hath commanded you? then thou shalt say unto thy son . . .

In other words, take advantage of those times when a child's curiosity factor is high. If God's Word is a normal and natural part of your daily conversation, your kids will catch on real quick. Remember, faith is caught as well as taught.

Teach Them Conspicuously

Teach the Word conspicuously (verses 8-9). The Jews took this so literally that they made little boxes called phylacteries, put the *Shema* in them, and tied them around their heads and on their wrists with a piece of leather.

Did God mean to do it that way? Perhaps He did. But what I think He meant was this: the Word "upon thine hand" reminds us that all we do is to be controlled by His Word. The Word "between thine eyes" reminds us that all we think is to be controlled by the Word of God.

Then Moses told God's people to write His Word on the doorposts of their houses. Again, the Jews did this by putting Scripture in a box or bag, called a mezuzah, and hanging it on their doorposts.

A box on your forehead or hand is pretty conspicuous. So is a box

on your doorpost. That's why during our series on the Ten Commandments at our church, we gave every family a beautiful parchment-like
copy of the Ten Commandments to frame and hang in their homes
and offices. Do whatever you can to make the Word of God evident in
your home.

If you will teach God's Ten Commandments convincingly, consistently, creatively, conversationally, and conspicuously, your children
will know that you really believe what you say you believe, and they'll
believe it too!

2

ONE GOD
PER FAMILY

*There is no other way because there is no other God. There
is one God, there is no God but God, and there is no rest for
any who rely on any god but God.*

—*Os Guinness and John Seel* [1]

A while back somebody gave me an interesting piece called "The
Mush God," written by Nicholas Van Hoffman. I'd like to share it
with you:

The Mush God has been known to appear to millionaires on golf
courses. He appears to politicians at ribbon-cutting ceremonies
and to clergymen speaking the invocation on national TV at
either Democratic or Republican conventions.

The Mush God has no theology to speak of, being a Cream
of Wheat divinity. The Mush God has no particular credo, no
tenets of faith, nothing that would make it difficult for believer
and nonbeliever alike to lower one's head when the temporary
chairman tells us that Reverend, Rabbi, Father, or Mufti, or So-
and-So will lead us in an innocuous, harmless prayer, for this
god of public occasions is not a jealous god. You can even invoke
him to start a hooker's convention and he/she or it won't be
offended.

God of the Rotary, God of the Optimists, Protector of the
Buddy System, The Mush God is the Lord of secular ritual, of the

necessary but hypocritical forms and formalities that hush the divisive and the derisive. The Mush God is a serviceable god whose laws are chiseled not on tablets but written on sand, open to amendment, qualification and erasure. This is a god that will compromise with you, make allowances and declare all wars holy, all peaces hallowed.

That's the Mush God. Have you ever met him? He's all around. This is the god that most Americans want to believe in—a god who makes no demands and issues no commands. With a god like this as our national deity, it's no wonder that youth leader Josh McDowell made a startling discovery when he asked thousands of church kids to respond to a survey containing seven statements about objective standards of truth and morality.

Their responses indicate that for the most part our Christian young people echo the world's view. For example, 57 percent of these young people could not even say there is an objective standard of truth. Some 85 percent agreed with the reasoning that says just because it's wrong for you doesn't mean it's wrong for me. And 55 percent of these young people—church kids—agreed that everything in life is negotiable. McDowell concludes that their ideas about right and wrong are "subject to change."[2]

What a job Satan is doing on the next generation. We need to ask the age-old question, "If the foundations be destroyed, what can the righteous do?" (Psalm 11:3). If our children don't learn to live within limits now, when will they?

A few years ago TV mogul Ted Turner announced that the Ten Commandments are obsolete. His comments were given wide publicity in the media. You may remember that he said the Ten Commandments don't relate to today's problems. They are outmoded rules. What we need, Turner said, is to substitute the Ten Commandments with what he called "Ten Voluntary Initiatives."

Set the results of Josh McDowell's survey next to the comments of a powerful man like Ted Turner, and you can see that we are in a nation today that needs to hear, "Thus saith the Lord." We need a sure word from God. That's why we're not talking about the Mush God.

We're talking about Jehovah God, the Creator who made it all, the God who thundered His Commandments from Sinai. We're talking about the God who will not share His glory with another. The "Perfect Ten" Commandments could only come from a perfect God.

In the opening chapter we laid a foundation for our study of the Ten Commandments, considering from Deuteronomy 6 what God expected from His people in Moses' day and what He expects from us as His people today. We talked about how we are to keep God's commands and how we are to teach them to the next generation. Now I want to begin building the superstructure on that foundation.

THE PRIORITY COMMANDMENT

The First Commandment rightly occupies the place of preeminence, the place of priority in the giving of the Commandments in Exodus 20. Obedience to this command should also occupy the place of priority in our lives today.

Notice that verse 1 says, "God spake *all* these words" (my emphasis). The Ten Commandments came from the mouth of the Lord Himself. This is revelation from on high; it is not human wisdom. The "tables of stone" were "written with the finger of God" (Exodus 31:18). These are not any human being's ideas or suggestions.

With all of this in mind, let's turn to the First Commandment:

> I am the LORD thy God, which have brought thee out of the land of Egypt, out of the house of bondage. Thou shalt have no other gods before me.
>
> —Verses 2-3

This is almost word for word identical with Deuteronomy 5:6-7, where Moses restates the Commandments as part of his farewell speech prior to Israel's entering the Promised Land. Before God told Israel what He wanted them to do, He told them who He was and what He had done for them (verse 2).

By delivering the children of Israel from bondage in Egypt, the Lord God had demonstrated His absolute superiority over all the false gods of Egypt. The ten plagues God sent upon Egypt struck at the heart of their pagan worship and showed their gods to be no gods at all. So God had every right to demand Israel's exclusive loyalty.

"I am the LORD thy God. . . . Thou shalt have no other gods before me." As I said in Chapter One, this is the great revelation of Scripture. There is only one Lord. All other so-called gods are merely the imaginations of men's minds or the deceptions of lying spirits.

You have to understand that this revelation of the one invisible, almighty God was, and still is, unique in history. The concept of a God who is pure spirit, who can neither be seen nor touched and who is wholly unlike us, was a radical departure from the pagan gods of antiquity.

The gods of the nations were always represented by an idol or some creature from nature, and they often merely reflected the sins and vices of their worshipers. But the true God is pure holiness, utterly separate from sin. And He is spirit (John 4:24). That's why He forbade Israel to make any likeness of Him, as we'll see when we get to the Second Commandment.

The God Whom Scripture Declares

Someone might say, "How do we know there is only one God?" Let me give you several important reasons. Number one, because Scripture declares the fact of God. By that I mean, the Bible presents the truth of God's existence as the first reality upon which everything else is built and depends.

You might think the First Commandment would say, "Thou shalt not be an atheist" or "Thou shalt not believe in atheism." But it doesn't say that. The Bible never even argues the issue of theism vs. atheism. God's Word just opens in Genesis 1:1 with the declaration, "In the beginning God . . ." Suddenly, sublimely, and surely the Bible presents us right up front with the fact of God.

What about atheism and all the other "isms" that deny the existence of God? Well, God gives them all the space they deserve. Did you know the Bible only devotes one half of one verse to atheism? Psalm 14:1 begins, "The fool hath said in his heart, There is no God."

That's it. That's all God's Word has to say about the atheist. In my preaching I don't try to prove the existence of God to people. I'm not writing this book to convince you that God is. That's not to say I don't ever deal with the evidence for God's existence from Scripture and from nature or that I don't try to persuade men and women to believe. I do ask for a decision.

What I mean is, I don't spend a lot of time trying to argue with someone who has already made up his mind that there is no God. The Bible calls that person a "fool," and you can't do much with a fool. In fact, I've learned never to argue with a fool in public. Onlookers won't be able to tell who's who.

What's the problem with a person like this? The problem is not that he *can't* believe. The problem is he *won't* believe. Notice that the psalmist says the atheist makes his decision in his heart, not in his head. A man who denies facts is a fool, and a man who denies the supreme fact is the supreme fool. The Scriptures declare the fact of God.

Have you ever noticed how simple it is to teach a little child about God? A child's heart is predisposed toward belief. That's why Jesus said that as adults we must not put stumbling blocks in the way of children coming to Him (Matthew 19:14).

But when you try to teach a child there is no God, the arguments become incredibly convoluted. One atheistic father was trying to teach his child that God doesn't exist. After he had finished his long, drawn-out explanation of how everything around us "just happened," the little child looked at his father and said, "Daddy, do you think God knows we don't believe in Him?" Belief in God is innate in the human heart.

The God Whom Creation Displays

Not only do the Scriptures declare the fact of God. The creation displays the hand of God. We talk about the laws of science by which the universe operates, but the fact is, they're not laws of science of all. They are the laws of God that science has only discovered and described. Scientists are no more capable of creating those laws than Christopher Columbus was capable of creating North America.

Columbus simply discovered a continent that was already there. Yet our children are being taught in school that they evolved from lower life forms, that they came up out of the primordial ooze. Worse yet, teachers cannot teach creation as a balance to the theory of evolution. And yet the Declaration of Independence says, "We hold these truths to be self-evident, that all men are created equal, that they are endowed by their Creator with certain unalienable Rights."

Something is wrong in our nation, which was built on the fact that we are the creation of God and are therefore endowed with certain rights. Today we cannot teach our children in public school that they were created by God. Instead, they're taught that billions of years of time plus chance brought life out of inorganic matter. Of course, the evolutionists still can't explain where that inorganic matter came from.

Even allowing for billions of years, evolution cannot turn frogs into princes. If you tell that story in nursery school, it's called a fairy tale. If you tell it in the classroom, it's called science. It's actually monkey mythology.

But this does not stop many scientists from taking an arrogant attitude toward anything they perceive as less than scientific. Dr. Hugh Ross, an eminent astrophysicist and Christian apologist, recalls this incident from his college days:

> The chauvinism of scientists is exemplified by a pep talk I heard in my undergraduate days at the University of British Columbia. "Not only can a good physicist do physics better than anyone else," said the professor, "he can do anything better than anyone else." He expressed the belief that science training is essential for grappling with the challenges of modern life. In a graduate course on relativity, my professor lamented theologians' past meddling in cosmology. "Today," he boasted, "we have been able to scare most of the ministers out of cosmology with a straightforward application of tensor calculus."[3]

Well, that professor and his colleagues may have scared a few ministers away from talking about creation and the origin of life, but they don't scare God! Dr. Ross said he later attended a theology colloquium where the speaker said that only theologians have the right to interpret all science since they are trained in "the mother of the sciences, theology." The speaker ended with this declaration: "Scientists have only observations. We have revelation!"[4]

Amen to that! For the heart and mind that is open and searching, every star and stone of creation reveals the glory and majesty of God.

The God Whom Faith Discovers

A third reason we know there is only one Lord is that we can discover the truth about Him by faith. Nobody has ever been argued into believing in God. That's because belief in God is not really an intellectual issue but a moral one.

People accuse Christians of being gullible believers in the unseen and the supernatural. Well, atheists are gullible believers in the seen and the natural. The fact is, everybody is a believer, including the atheist. He says to me, "Prove there is a God." I say I can't prove God to his satisfaction, so he just laughs. To him, I believe in something that cannot be demonstrated or proved.

But then I say to him, "Prove there is no God." He can't disprove God to my satisfaction either. That makes the atheist a believer too, because he also believes in something that cannot be demonstrated or proved.

You see, the atheist believes by faith that there is no God. I believe by faith that there is a God. The difference is, I believe with evidence. I have the external evidence of creation. And I have the internal evidence of the witness of God the Holy Spirit in my heart.

It comes down to this: if you want to believe in God, you can believe in God. As I said above, it is an issue not of the head, but of the heart. The fool of Psalm 14:1 isn't someone who has honest intellectual problems. There is evidence that can deal with those.

This person has moral problems, because he does not want God to rule over him. He does not want God telling him what to do. Like Ted Turner, this person says God's Commandments are obsolete because he wants them to be.

But God so created you that when your heart is right, it will respond to the fact of God the way a healthy eye responds to light or a healthy ear to sound. Your heart will respond to God when your heart is right before Him.

THE NECESSARY COMMANDMENT

So the great revelation is that there is one Lord and one God, the God of the Bible. The First Commandment forbids us from putting any other god before Him. That means there is to be no rival to God, no rebuttal to God, and no refusal of God.

The idea of "before me" is literally "before My face" or "in My sight." That is, God did not want Israel to bring any false god into His presence, either in addition to Him or in opposition to Him.

If Israel already knew the truth that there was only one true God, why did God deem it necessary to forbid the worship of other gods? Did Israel really need that prohibition? Consider this: during their 400 years of slavery in Egypt, the Israelites evidently became enamored with the Egyptian gods. And when they left Egypt, the people took with them a tendency toward idolatry that had been conceived in their hearts.

How do we know this? In Exodus 32 we read the painfully familiar account of the golden calf. The people got tired of waiting for Moses to come down from the mountain where he was receiving the Ten Commandments, so they had Aaron make them an idol of a calf or a young bull (verses 1-4).

Where do you suppose the children of Israel got the idea to make this golden calf? From their days in Egypt. And where do you suppose Aaron learned how to fashion this idol? He probably saw many of them being made in Egypt. And what did the people say of this false god? "These be thy gods, O Israel, which brought thee up out of the land of Egypt" (verse 4).

Israel broke the first two Commandments before they even knew what they were! This all sounds very much like today, when the idea of other gods is rampant. Our society is more like Egypt than Canaan. Our children are susceptible to false gods because they live in an Egypt-like culture. Most people don't need religion. In fact, they need to turn from religion to biblical Christianity.

It was only through the Babylonian Captivity and the destruction of Jerusalem and the temple that God was able to purge His people of much of their propensity to put other gods before Him. Will modern America, or even our own families, have to undergo a corresponding crisis to show us the frailty of false gods and bring us to the true God?

I thought of that when I was on an airplane one day and watched an Orthodox Jew having his private devotions. He got out his Scripture, and he began to read and nod his head.

But before he had done that, he took out his phylactery, his little Scripture box like the ones we talked about in Chapter One, and tied it around his head. Then he took Scripture and wrapped it around his right hand. He did not care who saw him or what I or anyone else might think; he was going to worship God.

Frankly, I was blessed as I watched that man. I long for him and other precious Jewish people to know God in the Person of His Son, the Lord Jesus Christ. But this Orthodox man was a reminder that Israel has been cured of the worship of false gods.

GOD'S COMMANDMENT FOR TODAY

"I am the LORD thy God. . . . Thou shalt have no other gods before me." This is still God's law for life today. It means that if I am obedient to Him, whatever He says, I will do. It means that I will allow nothing to come between me and my Lord, to take the place of absolute priority in my life that He deserves and demands.

Remember, God's commands are not for our punishment, but for our welfare. Even though eight of the Ten Commandments are negative, there is a positive implied in each one.

What God is saying is this: "give Me first place in your life." He loves you, so every time God says, "Thou shalt not," He's really saying, "Don't harm yourself." And every time God says, "Thou shalt," He's saying, "Help yourself to happiness."

We need to understand this principle. We must teach it to our children, and we have to begin early. Even though I don't agree with much that Roman Catholic educator Francis Xavier taught, he was right when he said, "Give me the children until they're seven, and anyone can have them afterward."

The prophet Isaiah writes:

> Whom shall he teach knowledge? and whom shall he make to understand doctrine? them that are weaned from the milk, and drawn from the breasts. For precept must be upon precept, precept upon precept; line upon line, line upon line; here a little, and there a little.
>
> —28:9-10

That's how you do it. Not all at once, but little by little as the children are able to receive and understand it. The key here is consistency, faithfulness. As I said in the opening chapter, we need to turn our homes into God's law schools and enroll our children. The primary professor is the father, and the curriculum is God's Ten Commandments.

God's Word still says, "Train up a child in the way he should go: and when he is old, he will not depart from it" (Proverbs 22:6). We are going to deal with this principle in the final chapter of the book, but I want to keep this great truth before you as we talk about obeying and teaching the Ten Commandments in our homes.

Of course, the best way to teach your children the truth of the First Commandment is to live it yourself in the home. If your kids see you putting other things ahead of God, they will become discouraged and disillusioned, like a young Jewish boy who once lived in Germany.

His father was a successful merchant, and the family practiced their Jewish faith. But then they moved to another German city, and the boy's father announced that they would no longer attend synagogue. They were going to join the Lutheran church.

The boy was very surprised and asked his father why the family was joining the Lutheran church. His father's answer was something like, "For business reasons. There are so many Lutherans in this town that I can make good business contacts at the Lutheran church. It will be good for business."

That boy, who had a deep interest in religion, became so disillusioned with his father that something died within him. He said to himself, "My father has no real convictions." The incident helped to turn him against religion with a vengeance.

That young boy later moved to England and began to write. His name was Karl Marx. As the father of communism he wrote the *Communist Manifesto*, in which he called religion "the opiate of the masses."

I wonder if world history would have been different had Karl Marx's father heeded the admonition of the great *Shema* of Israel:

> Hear, O Israel: The LORD our God is one LORD: and thou shalt love the LORD thy God with all thine heart, and with all thy soul, and with all thy might.
>
> —Deuteronomy 6:4-5

Your kids know whether you love God with all your heart. What they want to see is parents with such a love and reverence for God that they bring Him into every area of their lives and put Him first in everything. Kids want to see whether their parents love God enough to obey Him.

In the Upper Room, on the night of His betrayal, Jesus told the disciples, "If ye love me, keep my commandments" (John 14:15). He repeated this in verses 21 and 23, and again in John 15:10. The apostle John, who was present that night and heard Jesus' words, later wrote:

> By this we know that we love the children of God, when we love God, and keep his commandments. For this is the love of God, that we keep his commandments: and his commandments are not grievous.
>
> —1 John 5:2-3

True love for God always translates into obedience to Him. So the First Commandment tells us *whom* to worship: the Lord God, the one and only true God. The Second Commandment will tell us *how* to worship.

TURNING THE COMMANDMENTS INTO COMMITMENTS

0-6 Years

- Sing and talk about God with your children.
- Familiarize yourself with the videos and tapes available for young children.
- Read Bible stories to them.
- Help them thank God for food, friends, sunshine—everything.

7-12 Years

- Frame a copy of the Ten Commandments, and hang it in your children's room.
- Have your children memorize the Commandments, and reward them when they are successful.

- Practice daily family worship.
- Get your children their first Bible.
- Take them to a Christian bookstore, and let them select a tape or video they want.

13+ Years

- Get them a book that gives them reasons to believe—proofs of the truth of Christianity.
- Upgrade their personal Bible to a study Bible written especially for teens.
- Help your children begin taking responsibility for their own spiritual lives. Encourage them to have a daily quiet time.

3
—

LEARNING
FAMILY WORSHIP

Worship is giving to God the best He has given us.

—*Oswald Chambers*

I hope you're getting a clear message that God wants your home to succeed, not fail. But I also want you to understand that your home and mine will never succeed apart from learning and obeying the holy commandments of God, including the Ten Commandments. There is no possible way it can happen.

Why? Because as we have said, God's Ten Commandments are not arbitrary or temporary. They are for all people at all times. They are universally applicable.

In contrast, many of our society's laws are arbitrary. For example, in the United States we drive on the right side of the road. In England, they drive on the left side. I found out how arbitrary traffic laws are when I rented a car in London one time and tried to drive to northern England. I'll tell you, I was prayed up by the time I got there!

It really doesn't make much difference which side of the road you drive on, as long as everybody agrees. My point is that these laws are arbitrary. But the Ten Commandments are not arbitrary, and neither are they temporary. They don't need to be revised. They're not outmoded.

No one can logically add an eleventh Commandment. God put a period after the Tenth Commandment, and that period is still there.

That means you disregard the Ten Commandments at your own peril. People talk about breaking the Commandments. But in reality, you don't break them. They stand firm regardless of our response. "For ever, O LORD, thy word is settled in heaven" (Psalm 119:89). We don't break God's Commandments as much as we're broken on them.

A man who jumps out of a ten-story building doesn't break the law of gravity. He merely demonstrates it. And when you transgress God's Commandments, you are broken by them.

THE HOW OF WORSHIP

We saw in Chapter One that the Ten Commandments apply primarily to the home. From the home, then, they impact other spheres such as school, government, and business. But the home is primary. So let's take a careful look at the second of these great principles for the home:

> Thou shalt not make unto thee any graven image, or any likeness of any thing that is in heaven above, or that is in the earth beneath, or that is in the water under the earth: thou shalt not bow down thyself to them, nor serve them: for I the LORD thy God am a jealous God, visiting the iniquity of the fathers upon the children unto the third and fourth generation of them that hate me; and showing mercy unto thousands of them that love me, and keep my commandments.
>
> —Exodus 20:4-6

The First Commandment deals with the *who* of worship. The Second Commandment deals with the *how* of worship. The First Commandment forbids false gods. This Commandment forbids false worship, which also means it commands true worship because every negative has in it a positive, and every positive has in it a negative.

We're going to see this principle throughout our study. For instance, if I say to you, "Don't stay outside," that means, "Come inside." The only way you cannot stay outside is to come inside. So when the Bible issues an injunction against false worship, then, just as surely as night follows day, the Bible is commanding true worship.

So in reality the Second Commandment is a command that is meant to teach us true worship. Beyond the shadow of any doubt, the best thing you can do for your children is to teach them how to worship the true God. What a privilege, what a responsibility it is to teach family worship, to learn how to worship God together as a family.

Some years ago the incredibly gifted violinist Fritz Kreisler learned that an old Englishman possessed a Stradivarius violin, a very rare and beautiful instrument. Kreisler went to the old man and offered to buy it, but was told it was not for sale. Kreisler was rebuffed, but one day he went back to the old man's house and said, "If I can't buy the violin, may I touch it?"

The old Englishman invited him in. Kreisler picked up that rare and expensive violin, tucked it under his chin, and began to draw the bow across the strings. When he did, it was said you could hear the laughter of little children. You could hear babies crying. You could hear the birds singing in the trees. You could hear the voices of angels.

For about twenty minutes Kreisler played as only a master could play. As the old Englishman sat there, great tears began to well up in his eyes and course down his cheeks. When Kreisler saw that, he thought maybe he'd gone too far. He said, "I'm sorry, but I would so much like to buy this instrument."

The old Britisher said, "It is not for sale, but it is yours. You may have it! It belongs to you. You are the master. You alone are worthy of it."

That's what worship is all about. The Lord is the Master of the universe and of our lives, and He alone is worthy of our worship. You probably know that the word *worship* means to ascribe worth to something. God is worth all that we have and are. So I say, the best thing you can do for your children is not a college education, not an inheritance in the bank, and not vitamin-enriched food. Those are all good. But the best thing you can do for your kids is to teach them to worship.

Why? Because we become like the object of our worship. The Bible teaches us that when we worship an idol, we become like that idol. First the family molds the idol, and then the idol molds the family.

Everybody is going to worship something, because man is incurably religious. Nature abhors a vacuum. How important it is, therefore, that we learn to worship as God has commanded. The good news is that this principle of becoming like what we worship works positively too. That is, when we worship God, we become like Him.

A PROPER CONCEPTION OF GOD

As parents and teachers, it is our duty and privilege to give our children a proper conception of God. If you have a warped concept of God, you're going to have a warped worship and a warped life.

No Comparison

Idolatry is wrong because it gives a distorted or false picture of God. An idol is a material thing, and no idol can represent the invisible, spiritual God. Jesus said in John 4:24, "God is a Spirit." I know the *King James Version* includes the indefinite article, but the literal translation is, "God is spirit." That is, spirit is His very essence.

No wonder, then, that Jesus went on to say, "They that worship him must worship him in spirit and in truth." What material thing could possibly represent spirit? God is a circle whose center is everywhere and whose circumference is nowhere. God is spirit. There is nowhere where God is not, and no material thing can represent Him.

There's nothing you can compare God to or with. There's nothing that says, "This is what God is totally like." God Himself asked, "To whom then will ye liken me, or shall I be equal?" (Isaiah 40:25). We can say one man is like another man, one chair is like another chair, one piano like another piano, and so on. But there's only one God. You can't compare Him to anything or anyone.

That's the reason some people have difficulty with the doctrine of the Trinity. Someone says, "Well, I just don't understand it." That's all right. I wouldn't have any confidence in a God I could understand. Don't worry about trying to illustrate the Trinity. God says there is nothing like Him. And even if you could find something that was like God, you ought not to worship it.

Suppose a woman walks into a room and finds her husband embracing another woman. He sees his wife out of the corner of his eye and says, "Now wait a minute, honey. Don't get the wrong idea here. Let me tell you what I was doing. This woman is so beautiful, she reminded me of you. I was really just thinking of you when I was embracing her."

There's not a woman in America who would buy that, including my wife, Joyce! And God doesn't buy it either when we worship something else and say, "Now, Lord, wait a minute. Don't get the wrong idea here. I was only worshiping this thing because it reminds me of You. I'm really worshiping You."

No, you really aren't. That's what the Second Commandment is all about. "I the LORD thy God am a jealous God" (verse 5). Now, jealousy is to us an ugly word. We call it the "green-eyed monster." But there is a holy jealousy. You see, jealousy can be right or wrong. It all depends on whether it's warranted. For example, no athlete or singer has a right to be jealous of another athlete or singer, because they don't have a monopoly on athletics or music.

Underscore this thought in your mind and soul. *God has a monopoly on being God!* He has cornered the market. There's only one God, and His throne is not a duplex. God is not a part-time king. He is God! And He is "a jealous God." You have no right to worship anything or anybody but Him.

Modern Idols

We have just seen a proper conception of God. But not all idolatry consists of sticks and stones. Most Americans today don't make graven images. Very few of us have some molten god that we worship.

Martin Luther has well said that whatever your heart clings to and relies on, that is your god. Anything you love more than God, anything you fear more than God, anything you serve more than God, anything you value more than God is your god.

Did you know that idolatry is the greatest sin? Why? Because Jesus Himself said the greatest commandment is to love God with all of your heart and soul and mind (Matthew 22:37). Since idolatry breaks the greatest commandment, it must therefore be the greatest sin.

Why did God make us and set us in families? To love and worship Him. "For in him we live, and move, and have our being" (Acts 17:28). That is why we exist. Idolatry is really a renunciation of the whole purpose of life.

Now, you can have idols in your heart without making them with your hands. In America we have made gods of ourselves. "Me-ology" has replaced theology. Paul warned that in the last days men would be "lovers of their own selves" (2 Timothy 3:2), "whose God is their belly" (Philippians 3:19).

Some people have made a god of wealth. They worship at the shrine of money. Their god is gold. Their creed is greed. Their theology is, "Get all you can, and can all you get."

The evidence of this idolatry is easily seen. There are idolaters who will not unite with the church because they think membership may involve stewardship. But the Bible says that covetous people will not inherit the kingdom of God (1 Corinthians 6:10).

Some people even make a god of the family. Now, you ought to love your family. You should adore your family. I do mine. You ought to sacrifice for your family. But you dare not make a god of your family. I'm not writing to help you learn to put your family above everything else. Quite the contrary. I want to help you learn how to put God first in your family.

In fact, the worst thing you could do would be to put your family first—because whatever is first is your god. My wife, Joyce, knows she is not number one in my life. I know I'm not number one in her life, and I'm glad I'm not. We both desire to put God first in our affections and in our worship.

But because Joyce loves God supremely, she is able to love me with a love she could not give me if I were number one. And by being number two in her life, I'm loved more than I could ever be if I were number one.

This is so important to teach and to model before your children. They will be loved more if God is number one in your life than they could be if they were number one. Jesus Christ said, "He that loveth father or mother . . . son or daughter more than me is not worthy of me" (Matthew 10:37).

That may sound harsh, but this is where we start to separate those who think the Ten Commandments are just nice little rules from those who desire a radical but exciting faith.

You see, Jesus' call to put God first is demanding because God demands our best, our all. Obeying God's Ten Commandments is demanding—and delightful! Yet, putting Him first doesn't mean you love your family any less. It really means you love them more.

Other Americans have made gods of pleasures—chiefly sports. Paul said that in the last days men would be "lovers of pleasures more than lovers of God" (2 Timothy 3:4). Our sports stadiums and palaces of pleasure are filled. Sunday has become "Fun-day." The new Sunday ritual is professional football or other athletic highs.

I'm not saying that you have to choose between God and pleasure. "At [His] right hand there are pleasures for evermore" (Psalm 16:11). But pleasures cannot come first. If you're a lover of pleasure more than a lover of God, you are an idolater. I am what some would call a football fanatic, but my love for Jesus puts football in the shade.

You may remember when basketball great Michael Jordan gave up his try at baseball and returned to the Chicago Bulls. There's no denying Jordan's unique ability. In the realm of athletics, he deserves the accolade "great" or "superstar." What that man does with a basketball defies physics. He's in a class by himself.

But when Michael Jordan came back to professional basketball, the stock market went up. Can you believe it? I'm not trying to take anything away from him. He deserves honor as a world-class athlete. But the sad part of the story was the reaction of some people. Little kids were saying things like, "I have hope again." One sportswriter called Jordan's return "the second coming." It got so ridiculous that even Jordan said he was bothered by the comparison.

You know what's wrong in America today? We have too many idols and not enough heroes. We have sex idols and rock music idols and sports idols. But where are the heroes—the people worth admiring and emulating because of their character and integrity? One way you can help your children avoid this kind of idolatry is to help them find some real heroes and carefully examine their idols.

Idolatry and Art

Let me answer a question that always comes up whenever we deal with the Second Commandment. Does the prohibition against graven images include religious art? If you say yes, you're going to get yourself in serious trouble.

The Bible accepts religious art. The Old Testament tabernacle was itself a work of art. When Solomon built the temple according to the command of God, there were depictions of flowers, pomegranates, palm trees, oxen, and lions. Into the veil of the temple were woven beautiful figures. And guarding the mercy seat were the cherubim, artistic representations of angelic beings.

The Second Commandment does not forbid art. It forbids idolatry. John Calvin, the great Reformer, wrote that sculpture and painting are gifts of God. If art is your master, you're an idolater. But if art is your servant, it becomes your ministry.

God is the author of beauty, but He hates idolatry. To help our children understand the Second Commandment, we must first teach them a proper conception of God, then teach them the difference between pleasure and self-indulgence, between heroes and idols, between art and idolatry.

A PERSUASIVE COMMUNICATION OF GOD

There's a second thing that must be present if we are going to teach our children how to obey the Second Commandment—a persuasive communication of God.

A Stern Warning

Exodus 20:5 ends with a stern warning: "I the LORD thy God am a jealous God, visiting the iniquity of the fathers upon the children unto the third and fourth generation of them that hate me." God says that wrong worship is iniquity—sin.

Forget the idea that you can just choose however or whatever you want to worship without consequences. The iniquities of false worship show up in the children, grandchildren, and great-grandchildren of those who worship in a false way. That's the reason it is so tragic. God visits the iniquities of the fathers upon the children.

That doesn't mean God holds children guilty for their parents' sins. This is not talking about the guilt of the sin, but the tragic result of the sin. We see this in the natural realm. For example, when a mother-to-be is a user of crack cocaine, her baby is born with certain defects.

A Biblical Example

Let's consider a biblical story illustrating this principle and process in action, so you can see how important it is to teach your children the truth. In 2 Chronicles 26 we meet a godly and great king whose name was Uzziah. Verses 1-15 tell us that about him.

But one day Uzziah was filled with pride and decided he would worship God in his own way rather than in God's way. "But when [Uzziah] was strong, his heart was lifted up to his destruction: for he transgressed against the LORD his God, and went into the temple of the LORD to burn incense upon the altar of incense" (verse 16).

The following verses tell us that it was neither Uzziah's right nor his privilege to burn incense in the temple of God. What he did was false worship. No matter what his motive was, Uzziah attempted to worship God in the wrong way. He may have been sincere, but he was sincerely wrong.

The priests withstood Uzziah, but he got puffed up with anger, and in that instant God struck him with leprosy. At the end of verse 21 we find that "he was cut off from the house of the LORD: and Jotham his son was over the king's house, judging the people of the land." A father worshiped God in the wrong way, and now his son was going to take his place on the throne.

What was Jotham like? Well, 2 Chronicles 27:2 reveals that like his father Uzziah, Jotham "did that which was right in the sight of the LORD." But notice the last part of this verse: "Howbeit, [Jotham] entered not into the temple of the LORD. And the people did yet corruptly."

A pattern was beginning to take shape. Uzziah did not worship God in a proper way and was cut off from the house of the Lord. Then his son Jotham says, "Well, Dad had trouble down at that church, and he quit going. I don't see why I ought to go to church." (Of course, I'm using the term *church* here to put this in our terms today.)

So Jotham says, "Children, let's go down to the lake today and have a picnic. Bring your Bible along because we're going to have Sunday school down at the lake. We don't have to go to church to worship God. We don't have to worship God in a building with other people. My father loved God. He was a good man. I just think we'll have a little homemade religion." Jotham deliberately chose not to go to the house of God.

So far we have a father with *false worship* and a son with *neglected worship*. Now a grandson comes along. "And Jotham slept with his fathers, and they buried him in the city of David: and Ahaz his son reigned in his stead" (27:9).

What was Ahaz like? "He walked in the ways of the kings of Israel, and made also molten images for Baalim" (28:2). The Baalim were idols of Baal, the sex god. Now look in verse 24: "And Ahaz gathered together the vessels of the house of God, and cut in pieces the vessels of the house of God, and shut up the doors of the house of the LORD, and he made him altars in every corner of Jerusalem."

Can you believe that? This is the grandson of good King Uzziah! Uzziah loved God, but he misused the house of God. His son Jotham loved God, but he had no use for the house of God. But Jotham's son Ahaz worshiped idols. He destroyed the vessels of the temple and nailed the doors shut.

Think about your house of worship. I wonder if your grandchildren are going to close that place down and nail the doors shut. It's something to think about. It ought to be enough to motivate us to teach our children God's laws!

But this isn't over yet. It gets worse. Go back to verse 3 of chapter 28: "Moreover [Ahaz] burnt incense in the valley of the son of Hinnom, and burnt his children in the fire, after the abominations of the heathen whom the LORD had cast out before the children of Israel." Uzziah's grandson burned Uzziah's great-grandchildren to death as offerings to a horrible pagan god!

Molech was a heathen idol with outstretched arms and a hollowed-out belly in which was a great furnace of fire. His worshipers would heat Molech until he glowed and then sacrifice their babies to him by burning them in the fire.

You say, "No generation would destroy its children." Oh, really? Consider all the abuse and murder and abortion in our own land. Our hands drip with blood. We've learned that from the pagans, haven't we?

What a picture of the warning of Exodus 20:5 being carried out in judgment! Uzziah loved God, but he worshiped in a wrong way. Jotham loved God, but he had no use for the house of God. Ahaz hated the house of God and nailed the doors shut, then sacrificed his son to demon gods. What a tragedy!

A Godly Heritage

We're going to see the same thing happen to the children and grand-children of America if we don't get back to the true worship of Almighty God. I want my children and my grandchildren and my great-grand-children to love God. I'm standing on Psalm 112:2—"The generation of the upright shall be blessed."

"Well, it really doesn't make any difference what you do as long as it doesn't hurt anybody else." Have you ever heard that? Nobody ever sins solo; we are linked together. There is no such thing as sin only hurting one person. The hideous results of sin show up in the sinner's children.

But there's a positive side to this matter of influencing our children. Let's go back to the Commandments in Exodus 20: "For I the LORD thy God am a jealous God . . . showing mercy unto thousands of them that love me, and keep my commandments" (verse 5b-6).

Thank God for that promise. Not just three or four generations, but *thousands* of our descendants will be blessed if you and I will faithfully teach our children how to worship the true God.

We can each look down the corridor of time and say, "Dear God, I want to start something growing. Please start a fire in me that will never stop burning. I want my influence to go on and on and on."

I love what Paul said to Timothy: "I call to remembrance the unfeigned faith that is in thee, which dwelt first in thy grandmother Lois, and thy mother Eunice; and I am persuaded that [it is] in thee also" (2 Timothy 1:5). This legacy of faith started with the grandmother, went down to the mother, and then was handed down to Timothy.

That's the way it ought to be. A woman came to her pastor and asked, "When should I start the religious training of my child? When will he be old enough? Shall I start when he's six?"

Her pastor replied, "No, that's too late."

The woman responded, "Should I start when he's three years old?"

"No."

"At six months or one year old then?"

He said, "No that's still too late."

"When should I start then?" she finally asked.

"With his grandparents," her pastor replied.

Are you living for your grandchildren? Are you living with your great-grandchildren in view? "The generation of the upright shall be blessed."

A PRAYERFUL CELEBRATION OF GOD

Not only must there be a proper conception of God and a persuasive communication of God, but there must also be a prayerful celebration of God.

What I mean by this is that your children must see that your love for God is the most important thing in your life. You can't teach your children to love and obey God with passion if your love is lukewarm.

Do your children know that the most important thing to you is your love for God? If I were to ask your children, "What's the most important to your father? What's the most important thing in your mother's life?" what would they answer? I hope they would say, "Oh, that's easy. Our dad loves God with all of his heart. The most important thing on this earth to our mom is her relationship with God. Our parents love to worship Him."

It is imperative that we celebrate God in front of our children. This business of loving and serving God is not a matter of cold calculation. It's to be our passion, the consuming love of our hearts.

Our four grown children know that their parents are imperfect. No question about that. But they also know that we love God. I wouldn't be afraid for you to ask any one of them, "What's the most important thing to your dad and mom?" They would tell you that the most important thing to their parents is their relationship with God.

I really believe our children would say that. And I'm glad they would. I can't tell you how blessed I am to see them passing that love for God down to my grandchildren. What a privilege it is to worship God and to hand our lives over to Him the way that old Englishman handed his violin over to Fritz Kreisler, saying, "It belongs to you. You're the master, and you alone are worthy."

You cannot get someone else excited about something that makes you yawn. I like the way Howard Hendricks puts it: "If you want other people to bleed, you're going to have to hemorrhage." If you really believe that God alone is worthy of your worship, and if you love and worship Him with all your heart, your children will catch the fever. We must teach them and show them the truth of the Second Commandment.

TURNING THE COMMANDMENTS INTO COMMITMENTS

0-6 Years
- Talk about the idea of an invisible God, helping your children to understand the difference between imaginary and invisible.
- Let your kids hear you expressing praise and adoration to the Lord.
- Explain how the pictures in their Bible story books got there— for example, explain that pictures of Jesus are just the artists' ideas of what Jesus may have looked like.

7-12 Years
- Help your children put this Commandment into their own words.
- Help them pick out worthy heroes (missionary biographies are a great source for this).
- Find pictures of religious idols, ancient or current, to use as a discussion starter.
- Warn your children about the occult.

13+ Years
- Introduce your children to good Christian art if you haven't already done so.
- Offer to listen to their music with them, and evaluate it together.
- Watch for events in the news to discuss with your kids, especially stories that reveal people "worshiping" wealth, power, fame, or some other modern idol.

4

THE NAME ABOVE ALL NAMES

One day all creation shall bow to our Lord;
E'en now, 'mong the angels his name is adored.
May we at his coming, with glorified throng,
Stand singing his praises in heaven's great song:
"Jesus, Jesus, Savior adored,
Of all men and angels forever the Lord."

—*Dutch hymn* [1]

An old song tells us to "accentuate the positive" and "eliminate the negative." But frankly, that's silly. There can be no positive if we eliminate the negative. Without the negative, in fact, we would not even know what the positive looked like.

Did you ever stop to think why so many of the Ten Commandments are stated in the negative? Is it because God is negative? No. Is it because He wants to see us and our families fail or to constantly tell us what we're doing wrong? Of course not.

God wants your family to succeed! The bottom line of all the Commandments is this: God loves us. His Commandments are not rules to make us squirm like a worm in hot ashes as we try to keep them. These laws are for our good and our welfare.

As I said before, every time God says, "Thou shalt not," He's simply saying, "Don't hurt yourself." And every time God says, "Thou shalt," He's saying, "Help yourself to some happiness." If God says don't do the negative, He infers that we are to do the positive. If He says do the positive, He infers that we are not to do the negative.

So I say, don't think negatively about the Commandments. Not long ago I was talking with my friend Dr. James Dobson, who said something very interesting along this line.

"Adrian, you know that the battery in your car has negative and positive poles. If you put your hand on the negative pole alone, it won't bother you. Put your hand on the positive pole alone, and it won't bother you. But connect them together and grab hold, and it will curl your hair."

WHAT'S IN A NAME?

It takes the negative and the positive together to give the power. That's the reason God has given these Ten Commandments as they are. Let's now consider the Third Commandment:

> Thou shalt not take the name of the LORD thy God in vain: for the LORD will not hold him guiltless that taketh his name in vain.
>
> —Exodus 20:7

God tells us not to take His name in vanity. That infers we are to take His name in victory. This is the approach we'll follow.

What's in a name? That question has been asked many times. What's so important about a name? Well, in Bible times when a child was born, the parents would pray over that child and give him or her a name that encompassed a prayer and a prophecy concerning that child.

That's the reason we see so many people in the Bible whose names match their character. Jesus is the perfect example. He came to be the Savior of the world, so the angel said to Joseph, "Thou shalt call his name JESUS: for he shall save his people from their sins" (Matthew 1:21). The name "Jesus" means "Jehovah saves." Names had great meaning in the Bible, so it's very important that we understand what is conveyed in the name of Jehovah.

Personality in the Name

First of all, there's personality in that name. The God we serve is not some abstraction, not some kind of *Star Wars* impersonal force. He is a real Person, the self-named One, "the LORD thy God." When the word LORD is written in all capital and small capital letters, you are reading a translation of the Hebrew word *Jehovah* or *Yahweh*. This is the most personal name of God. He is saying to us, "I am Jehovah. I am a Person. Let Me introduce Myself to you."

By giving Himself names God is saying, "This is who I am. Learn My personality from My name. It tells what I am like." The name *Jehovah* speaks of the God who is a covenant-keeper. It signifies God's personal relationship to His people. He is the God who keeps His Word. Who wants to worship a God you could not trust to keep His promises?

Power in the Name

There is also power in that name. The Hebrew word *Elohim*, translated "thy God," speaks of a God who is the Mighty One. It is a plural word, because it speaks of the multiplicity of His strength and power.

Put these two names together and you get a picture of the God who says, "Be careful how you use My name. I am the covenant-keeping God who has the power to perform His Word. I am the God who will never break His promises to you. I am Jehovah your Elohim, the LORD your God. Don't take My name in vain."

Remember when David came against Goliath, the original Bigfoot (1 Samuel 17)? I mean, he was big and tough. And he was defying the armies of Israel. Everybody else was afraid to fight him.

But little David volunteered to go out against Goliath. David tried that tin can called Saul's armor, but discarded it and took just his sling and a few stones and went on out to meet Goliath. When the giant saw him coming, he was angry because it was an insult to a great warrior like him to have a young boy sent out against him.

The Bible says David was just a lad, "ruddy" with a "beautiful countenance" (1 Samuel 16:12). I take that to mean he had peach fuzz on his chin. He hadn't started to shave yet; he was just a teenager. Here he comes, a shepherd boy with his sling. Notice Goliath's reaction:

> And when the Philistine looked about, and saw David, he disdained him: for he was but a youth, and ruddy, and of a fair countenance. And the Philistine said unto David, Am I a dog, that thou

comest to me with staves? And the Philistine cursed David by his
gods. And the Philistine said to David, Come to me, and I will give
thy flesh unto the fowls of the air, and to the beasts of the field.

—1 Samuel 17:42-44

Here's a loose translation of Goliath's threat: "Sonny boy, when I get
my hands on you, I'm going to break you in pieces and feed you to the
pigeons."

I love David's reply: "Then said David to the Philistine, Thou comest
to me with a sword, and with a spear, and with a shield: but I come to
thee in the name of the LORD of hosts, the God of the armies of Israel,
whom thou hast defied" (verse 45). Then David hit Goliath square in the
forehead with that stone.

Goliath was surprised. It was the first time anything like that had
ever entered his head! He went down, and David took his sword and cut
off the giant's head. This is probably the greatest single victory in the history of warfare. Where did David get the power to accomplish it? "In the
name of the LORD of hosts." There is power in the name of our Lord.

Jesus said in John 14:14, "If ye shall ask any thing in my name, I will
do it." In Colossians 3:17 Paul reminds us, "And whatsoever ye do in
word or deed, do all in the name of the Lord Jesus." We're to do everything in the power of His name. That means you should go to work in His
name. Do your homework in His name. Rear your children in His name.
You say, "Do I take that literally?" Well, that's what the Bible says. That's
how all-encompassing the name of the Lord Jesus is.

Protection in the Name

But not only is there personality and power in the name of the Lord—
there is also protection in His name. Proverbs 18:10 tells us, "The name
of the LORD is a strong tower: the righteous runneth into it, and is safe."

Is Satan after you? Head for the name of Jesus. Take refuge in His
name. I love the old hymn that says:

> *Take the name of Jesus with you,*
> *Child of sorrow and of woe.*
> *It will joy and comfort give you.*
> *Take it then where'er you go.*

If temptations 'round you gather,
Breathe that holy name in prayer.

There is protection in the precious name of Jesus. When you breathe His holy name in prayer, it's like running into a strong tower for safety. And you can see things from that tower that you couldn't see from any other place because there you have a wonderful perspective.

Provision in the Name

There is also wonderful provision in the name of Jesus. We read in John 16:23-24 that our Lord said, "And in that day ye shall ask me nothing. Verily, verily, I say unto you, Whatsoever ye shall ask the Father in my name, he will give it you."

That means anything you can sign Jesus' name to, you can have. But the key is asking in Jesus' name—not in your name or simply to fulfill your desires. But if Jesus wants you to have it, you can sign His name to the order slip, and God the Father will give it to you.

Praise in the Name

When you understand that there is personality, power, provision, and protection in the name of the Lord, you understand why praise ought to be offered in His name as well. What could be more comely for God's people than to praise the name of the Lord Jesus? The psalmist cries out, "O LORD our Lord, how excellent is thy name in all the earth!" (Psalm 8:1). "O magnify the LORD with me, and let us exalt his name together" (Psalm 34:3). What a privilege it is to praise God in the name of Jesus!

HOW *NOT* TO TAKE HIS NAME

With all of that in mind, let's consider two important things when it comes to teaching our children the Third Commandment. We must teach them how not to take God's name in vanity, and we must help them take His name in victory. If we teach this in our homes, we are on the road to success.

We're not to take the name of the Lord our God "in vain." What does that mean? Well, the Hebrew word means meaningless, empty of content. It has its root in the idea of a tempest or storm. The Hebrews used the word to describe a storm because it seemed so random, with no rhyme or reason. It was erratic, just a worthless and nonproductive thing. You can see why after a while the word came to mean vain, careless, or thoughtless.

Can you imagine anything more out of touch with the character of God than to take His name in vain? The one who does so incurs guilt. So let's talk about teaching your children to beware of the vain use of the name of God.

The Vanity of Profanity

The first thing you need to teach your children is never to use profanity.

One of the most ignorant things a person could ever do is profane the name of God. When you use God's name in profanity, it shows two things: an empty head and a wicked heart. You see, profanity reveals a feeble mind trying to express itself. But it also reveals a wicked heart truly expressing itself. "Out of the abundance of the heart the mouth speaketh," Jesus said in Matthew 12:34.

A profane mouth reveals a profane heart. Profanity using the name of God is an insult flung into His face. It's so needless and unproductive, whereas other sins at least gain something (though not anything good). I'm not saying a person ought to commit murder for revenge, but at least he gets revenge. I'm not saying a person ought to steal if he has a need, but at least he gets what he steals. But what does a person get when he takes God's name in vain? Only judgment.

A fish might bite a hook that has no bait on it, but what does that accomplish? Similarly, taking God's name in vain is an utterly pointless and excuseless sin. What contempt it shows for Almighty God. We often hear people asking God to damn another person even though Jesus suffered in agony and blood to save people. What a profane perversion of prayer it is to ask God to send somebody else to hell.

You say, "Adrian, we've got this one down. Our family doesn't use that kind of language." That's wonderful. May I ask you a question? Do you permit secondhand swearing? I am referring to words such as darn, dang, gosh, and jeez.

"Oh," you say, "those are just euphemisms. They're just substitutes." Yes, they certainly are. "Gosh" is a substitute for the name God. "Jeez" is a substitute for the precious name of Jesus. And "darn" is simply a substitute for "damn." A lot of people would be surprised if they knew what they were really saying when they said, "Gosh darn you." We need to be careful with our speech. Don't use even secondhand swearing or your kids might get the idea that profanity isn't all that bad.

I can tell you there's at least one man somewhere in America today who has been cured of using God's name in a profane way. According to author Jerry Jenkins, this man had an encounter one day with the late Paul Anderson, a dear friend of mine who was known as "the strongest man in the world."

Paul won the Olympic Gold Medal in weightlifting in 1956. One of his many feats of strength is cited in the *Guinness Book of World Records*—lifting more than three tons with his back! He was only 5 feet 9 inches tall, but he weighed 375 pounds. He looked a little pudgy, but he was a slab of steel. He was incredibly strong.

Paul Anderson loved God with all of his heart. One day he was in an airport, and he heard a man use the name of Jesus Christ with an angry voice. Paul came up behind him, wrapped his arms around the man, and lifted him high in the air, asking excitedly, "Where is He? He's a friend of mine!"

When this poor guy saw who was holding him, he cried out, "Oh, my God!"

Paul said, "That's Him. Where is He?" I don't know what happened to that fellow, but I'll bet you he thought a long time before he ever took God's name in vain again![2]

One of these days God's going to put His arms around some of us and say, "Why did you take My name in vain? I'm your God—the God of the universe." What will we say then?

The Vanity of Frivolity

Profanity is certainly one way to violate God's Third Commandment. But did you know that this Commandment is not concerned primarily with swearing? That's as far as most of us go with it. But there's another way you can take God's name in vain, and that's by frivolity—just using the name of God carelessly or lightly. Many of us do this much more than we use profanity.

But God says don't do it. "But fornication, and all uncleanness, or covetousness, let it not be once named among you, as becometh saints; neither filthiness, nor foolish talking, nor jesting" (Ephesians 5:3).

What does Paul mean by "foolish," "jesting" talk? It's all those little sayings, the flippant little phrases we use that include the holy name of God. How carelessly we may say, "God bless you" or "Oh, Lord."

If we mean it, that's fine. But if it's just a little witticism or an offhand remark, that's something else.

A man once told me what he thought was a funny story about the Lord Jesus playing golf in heaven and always making a hole-in-one. I didn't think it was funny. I never think pointless jokes about God are funny. Using good humor to illustrate a point is fine, but jesting about God goes beyond humor.

If the Third Commandment warns us against using God's name in frivolity, then why would we want to do it? It's as repugnant to God to take His name in frivolity as it is in profanity. So the best thing to teach your children is to never ever use God's name unless they're serious.

The Vanity of Hypocrisy

There's a third way that God's name is often used in vanity, and that's in hypocrisy. I don't believe anything turns teenagers off more than hypocrisy in the home. When Mom and Dad do not live what they profess, it doesn't matter how active they are at church. The kids see right through them.

> Hear ye this, O house of Jacob, which are called by the name of Israel, and are come forth out of the waters of Judah, which swear by the name of the LORD, and make mention of the God of Israel, but not in truth, nor in righteousness.
>
> —Isaiah 48:1

What a picture of hypocrisy—people who make mention of God's name, but not in truth or righteousness.

This is why so many teenagers say, "I'm sick and tired of church. My dad and mom go down there. They teach a Sunday school class. He leads in prayer. He takes the offering. She sings in the choir. But at home they're phonies." That's taking the name of the Lord in hypocrisy.

Jesus said, speaking of the day of judgment, "Many will say to me in that day, Lord, Lord, have we not prophesied in thy name? and in thy name have cast out devils? and in thy name done many wonderful works? And then will I profess unto them, I never knew you: depart from me, ye that work iniquity" (Matthew 7:22-23).

If you're going to live for God, live for God in your home. And when you take the name of Jesus on your lips, do not use that wonderful name in hypocrisy. Let your yes be yes and your no no. Let your children know beyond the shadow of any doubt that you love Him. When you pray in the name of Jesus, don't just forge His name onto the end of the prayer. That's a hypocritical prayer. When you praise God, do it with all of your heart.

You know, sometimes we even sing our hypocrisy when we come to church. For instance, we sing, "My Jesus, I love Thee, I know Thou art mine; for Thee all the follies of sin I resign." Do you sing that and yet harbor sin in your heart? We sing, "Take my silver and my gold, not a mite would I withhold." Yet we hold on to our money with all of our might. "Faith of our fathers, holy faith, we will be true to thee 'til death." But we think nothing of skipping church if company comes. "All to Jesus I surrender, all to Him I freely give." If you don't mean that when you sing it, you're not much different from a man who curses and swears.

So you can take the name of God in vain by using it in profanity, in frivolity, or in hypocrisy. That's the negative side of this Third Commandment. I don't need to say any more on this except to remind you that "the LORD will not hold him guiltless that taketh his name in vain."

HOW TO TAKE HIS NAME

Now let's turn this thing over, because in the negative there is a wonderful positive: taking God's name in victory. I'd much rather you teach your children how to take His name in victory because when they learn to do that, they will certainly not want to take His name in vanity.

How do you take God's name in victory? I think the answer lies in Colossians 3:17—"And whatsoever ye do in word or deed, *do all in the name of the Lord Jesus*" (emphasis mine). That's taking His name in victory.

Do you know what the last name given for God in the Bible is? It is *Jesus*, the wonderful name that means "Jehovah saves." It is the most precious word to me in all of the Bible.

A friend in our church in Memphis gave me a framed copy of a poem that I have hanging by the door in my office. It's called "The Name" and is written by Henry W. Frost. Just before I go out to preach, I stop frequently and read this poem. I'd like to share it with you because it's one of the most beautiful things I've ever read:

> *There is a name, a wondrous name*
> *Of infinite and endless fame,*
> *Of God beloved, by saints revered,*
> *By angels and archangels feared,*
> *Ordained by God ere world began,*
> *Revealed by angels unto man,*
> *Proclaimed by men, believed, adored*
> *By hearts in prayer and praise outpoured.*
> *The theme of prophet, priest, and king,*
> *The word of which sweet psalmists sing,*
> *By pilgrims blessed, by suff'rers sung,*
> *The last word breathed by martyr's tongue,*
> *The name most precious and sublime,*
> *Supreme in space, supreme in time,*
> *Destined to live and conquer all*
> *Till all knees everywhere shall fall*
> *And tongues confess—what God proclaims—*
> *This name to be the Name of names,*
> *The name which in high heaven will be*
> *The One Name of eternity;*
> *Then, O my soul, its praise forthtell,*
> *Jesus the Name ineffable!*

This is our Lord and Savior, Jesus Christ, the One who invites us to take His name on our lips in victory! I'm not ashamed to tell you that sometimes the tears well up in my eyes as I read these words and think of the wonderful, wonderful name of Jesus. All of the names of God are compressed in that name that is above every name—the name of Jesus.

What do you need to teach your children about the Third Commandment in order to have a successful home? How can you help your kids learn to take God's name in victory? There are three things I tried to teach my children, and I encourage you to teach these to your children as well.

Wear the Name

Teach your children to wear the name. According to Acts 11:26, "The disciples were called Christians first in Antioch." When we call ourselves Christians, we are wearing the very name of Christ. Paul wrote in 2 Timothy 2:19, "Nevertheless the foundation of God standeth sure, having this seal, The Lord knoweth them that are his. And, Let every one that nameth the name of Christ depart from iniquity."

Believe it—when you call yourself a Christian and you name the name of Christ, you are wearing His name. But to do that successfully, you've got to walk the walk.

When my children were little, I used to drive them to school. I always looked forward to that time. I'd try and get my work, breakfast, and quiet time done so I could put the kids in the car and enjoy some special time as I drove them to school.

Invariably morning after morning just as they would get out of the car I would say to them, "Children, remember who you are and Whose you are." And I didn't mean, "Remember, you belong to me." I was saying, "Remember who you are—you're Christians. And you belong to Jesus Christ. You're not your own. You were bought with a price." I wanted my children to remember that they were wearing the name of Jesus when they went to school.

Share the Name

I also urge you to teach your children to share the name. Malachi 3:16 is one of the grandest verses in the Bible.

> Then they that feared the LORD spake often one to another: and the LORD hearkened, and heard it, and a book of remembrance was written before him *for them that feared the LORD, and that thought upon his name.* (emphasis mine)

Isn't that wonderful? God is so pleased when we even think on His name in victory that He has His angels record it in a book of remembrance. Imagine what it will do for your child's heart to know that he or she can make God so happy that He just has to stop and write it down!

But here's more. If you want a family Bible study that will be unforgettable, tell your kids about God's three books. He has the book of His revelation (that's the Bible). He has the book of redemption (that's "the Lamb's book of life," Revelation 21:27). And then He has the book of remembrance for those who fear Him and think upon Him.

Challenge your kids to make sure they are in all three of God's books. They can write their name under the "whosoever" of John 3:16, a key verse in God's written revelation. They can write their name in the Lamb's book of life by receiving Jesus as their Savior. And they can get their name in God's book of remembrance by taking His name in victory.

God keeps a book of remembrance for those who fear His name—for those, we could say, who keep the Third Commandment. Before we leave Malachi 3:16, look at all that is involved in this marvelous verse. Here is the godly *character* we should be building into our children.

You see, when a person takes God's name in vain, it's because he doesn't fear the Lord. The greatest mark of character is the fear of the Lord. "The fear of the LORD is the beginning of knowledge" (Proverbs 1:7). A nation is on its last legs when it no longer fears God.

That's the character you should teach your children—to fear the Lord. But notice also in Malachi 3:16 the *contemplation* they should practice—to think upon His name. If you want to teach your children something wonderful, teach them the names of God.

Teach them, for example, that *Jehovah tsidkenu* means "the Lord our righteousness." Teach them that *Jehovah shalom* means "the Lord our peace." Tell them about *Jehovah nissi*, "the Lord our banner." Teach them that *Jehovah shammah* means "the Lord who is present." Remind them that *El Shaddai*, "the Almighty One," is the God who stands watch over them each night.

What a wonderful study for your family devotions—the names of our God. Teach your children to know the names of God, and something marvelous will happen. Psalm 9:10 puts it this way: "They that know thy name will put their trust in thee."

Notice also the *conversation* of those who thought on the Lord's name. "They . . . spake often one to another." What were they talking about? It's obvious that they were talking about His name. When we come to church, we need to talk about the Lord Jesus, not about sports or the weather. As we read above in Psalm 34:3, the Bible calls us to "exalt his name together."

When we come to church, we're also to be exhorting one another (Hebrews 10:25). When we gather together, somebody will be down, but somebody else will be up. Somebody will have a question, but somebody else will have an answer. Somebody will be discouraged, but somebody else will be encouraged and encouraging.

So we exalt the Lord's name together, and we exhort one another. We talk about our Lord in song and in conversation. So many people are putting His name down, let's teach our children how to exalt God—to lift Him up. It's all part of sharing His name.

Bear the Name

Finally, teach your children to bear His name. It won't be easy. Did you know that the name of Jesus is hated more than any other name on the face of this earth? It's hard to believe, isn't it? His name is loved more than any other name on earth, but it's also hated more than any other.

So don't get the idea that when you wear and share the name of Jesus you won't have any reproach. Acts 5:40-42 puts that notion to rest.

The apostles had been preaching in the name of Jesus. They were arrested, dragged before the Sanhedrin, and beaten for preaching Jesus. But notice their reaction: "They departed from the presence of the council, rejoicing that they were counted worthy to suffer shame for his name. And daily in the temple, and in every house, they ceased not to teach and preach Jesus Christ" (verses 41-42).

There is a concerted effort against the name of Jesus, but we must bear His name. One of the men I admire deeply for this is George Beverly Shea, Billy Graham's longtime associate and baritone soloist.

Many years ago I was at a breakfast at an Air Force base. I was sitting on the dais next to George when a man came up and said to him, "Would you sing for us?"

Bev Shea said, "I'd be happy to."

"Could you sing 'How Great Thou Art?'" the man asked. Bev said that would be fine.

Then the man leaned closer to Mr. Shea and said, "You know, we have some people here today who are not Christians. Could you just leave out that verse that says 'God His Son not sparing'?"

I heard the man's request, and I was wondering what Mr. Shea would say to that. In the sweetest way he replied, "Oh, no, I couldn't leave that out. That would be to deny my Lord. It's all right. I just won't sing."

The man said, "Oh, well, it's all right. You can sing about Jesus." George Beverly Shea thanked him, stood up there, and sang about his Lord and Savior Jesus Christ.

I'll never forget that. This is what it means to teach your children to bear the name of Jesus—to unfurl and march under the blood-stained banner of Prince Emmanuel. Don't be ashamed of the One who died for you. Bear the name in victory.

I read somewhere that when he was on his deathbed, General William Booth, that great and godly man who founded the Salvation Army, was approached by family members who said, "Daddy, before you go to see Jesus, it would help a lot if you'd just sign your name here, so we can avoid business difficulties later."

The old man said that would be fine. So they put the paper before him, put a pen in his hand, and he signed. Not long afterward, General Booth stepped into glory. When the family opened that document, do you know what they saw? He had not signed his own name but had just written "Jesus." That was the name on his heart even more than his own.

The Bible says that God has given Jesus "a name which is above every name: that at the name of Jesus every knee should bow . . . and every tongue should confess that Jesus Christ is Lord, to the glory of God the Father" (Philippians 2:9-11).

One day very soon we are going to see the King. On that great day, we will be so glad we learned to take God's name in victory and not in vain and that we taught our children to do the same.

TURNING THE COMMANDMENTS INTO COMMITMENTS

0-6 Years

- Make sure your little ones have plenty of good music that praises and exalts the name of Jesus.

- Make an early vow that you and your mate will be careful how you use the name of God in your everyday conversation.

- Help your children make little banners with the names and titles of Jesus on them and decorate them with crowns or whatever symbol is appropriate to that name.

- Teach your children to pray in Jesus' name, and tell them what that means.

- Consider starting a "book of remembrance" on each child that highlights important moments in their spiritual lives such as their salvation and baptism.

7-12 Years

- Teach your children the names of God, beginning with the names in this chapter. Your Christian bookstore has books containing all the biblical names of God.

- Help your children apply the names of God to their personal needs: fear of harm, guilt for wrong behavior, etc.

- Continue with age-appropriate music that lifts up the name of Jesus.

13+ Years

- Be careful not to joke about God with your children.

- Remind your children why you chose their names, what their names mean, and the value you place on their names and on them. Tie your discussion to the value God places on His name.

- Regularly encourage your teenagers to wear the name of Jesus well as they go to school or other activities.

5

HOW TO MAKE THE REST DAY THE BEST DAY

God has not bowed to our nervous haste nor embraced the methods of our machine age. The man who would know God must give time to Him.

—*A. W. Tozer*

In this day when we're supposed to have so many devices to save time, I've never seen so many hurried and restless people! If the computer, the calculator, the cellular phone, and all of these other technological wonders are supposed to save us time, why do we have so little time for the things that matter?

It seems that with all we've accomplished, about all we have really added is speed and noise. We get there faster, but we don't know where we're going. And when we get there, we're out of breath.

I read one time about a man who swallowed an egg whole. He was afraid to move because he was afraid it would break. But he was afraid to sit still because he was afraid it would hatch. There are a lot of people like that today—so frenetic, so pressured they don't know which way to go. And the place where the pressure and the restlessness often hit home is in the home.

Homes today are places of upheaval. There used to be a time when a man would come home, put his hat down, wipe his brow, and say, "Boy, it's good to be home. It's a jungle out there." Today the jungle is on the inside.

God's Cure for Restlessness

But God has given us a cure for restlessness in the home, and therefore for peace outside the home. God has given us a day of rest. Many of us don't use it, and we don't even really know much about it. But God gave a wonderful gift to us in the Fourth Commandment:

> Remember the sabbath day, to keep it holy. Six days shalt thou labor, and do all thy work: but the seventh day is the sabbath of the LORD thy God: in it thou shalt not do any work, thou, nor thy son, nor thy daughter, thy manservant, nor thy maidservant, nor thy cattle, nor thy stranger that is within thy gates: for in six days the LORD made heaven and earth, the sea, and all that in them is, and rested the seventh day: wherefore the LORD blessed the sabbath day, and hallowed it.
>
> —Exodus 20:8-11

The sabbath day was God's gift given first to His ancient people, the nation of Israel. Jesus Himself told us in Mark 2:27 that "the sabbath was made for man, and not man for the sabbath." In reality, all of the Ten Commandments were made for us. That's why I said they are God's way of saying, "Don't hurt yourself" and "Help yourself to some happiness."

Let me also remind you that God did not give us the Ten Commandments to make us squirm like a worm in hot ashes trying to keep them. God's laws are for our welfare.

We'll see just how true that is in this chapter, because I want to show you something tremendous. As great a gift as the Old Testament sabbath was to Israel, God has given us something even better today—namely, the Lord's day, which is the transformation and fulfillment of the sabbath into something even more blessed.

As a Christian family, you have been given a special day of rest that, if you'll use it properly and enjoy it as you should, will be one of the best and richest jewels in your treasure chest of family values.

The very word *sabbath* means "rest." In fact, our English word is simply a transliteration of the Hebrew word for rest, *shabbat*. There are actually three primary rest days in the Bible. They are creation rest, covenant rest, and Calvary rest. If you can keep these days sorted out in your mind, you'll keep your reins untangled as we study the Fourth Commandment. Let's deal with these one at a time.

Creation Rest

What is God's creation rest? Well, verse 11 of our text makes that clear. When God finished creating the world in six days, He rested. Moses recorded the event in Genesis 2:1-3:

> Thus the heavens and the earth were finished, and all the host of them. And on the seventh day God ended his work which he had made; and he rested on the seventh day from all his work which he had made. And God blessed the seventh day, and sanctified it: because that in it he had rested from all his work which God created and made.

God made the world in six days, and then He rested. Was He tired? Of course not. God never gets weary (Isaiah 40:28). He rested for the same reason there are rests in music. It's not because the musicians are tired, but because they want to have a pause for emphasis and reflection—to rejoice in what has just gone before and to let it sink in.

But God's creation rest has been disturbed. What interrupted God's rest and put Him back to work? The entrance of sin. In John 5:1-16 Jesus healed a man on the sabbath day, the day of rest. The Pharisees, in whom the milk of human kindness had curdled, condemned Him for working on the sabbath day.

Take special note of Jesus' answer to them: "My Father worketh hitherto, and I work" (verse 17). God's creation rest has been disturbed by sin, and until sin is fully and finally banished from His creation, there is work to do.

Covenant Rest

The next day of rest the Bible talks about is covenant rest. Creation rest pertained to God Almighty. Covenant rest pertained to the nation of Israel. God gave His special covenant people a special day of rest—the seventh day, the day we call Saturday, the last day of the week:

Speak thou also unto the children of Israel, saying, Verily my sab-
baths ye shall keep: for it is a sign between me and you throughout your generations; that ye may know that I am the LORD that
doth sanctify you. . . . Wherefore the children of Israel shall keep
the sabbath, to observe the sabbath throughout their generations, for a perpetual covenant. It is a sign between me and the
children of Israel for ever.

—Exodus 31:13, 16-17a

Notice that God gave His covenant rest to a particular people, the Jews. The Old Testament sabbath, the seventh day of the week, was to be a sign of the covenant between God and the children of Israel.

Some people today say we should observe the sabbath day—that is, Saturday—the way the people in the Old Testament kept it. We must be very careful about claiming we keep the sabbath. To break an Old Testament sabbath law in Israel meant sudden death. Remember, Israel was a theocracy. The people lived under the direct rule of God.

Look at verse 15 of Exodus 31: "Six days may work be done; but in the seventh is the sabbath of rest, holy to the LORD: whosoever doeth any work in the sabbath day, he shall surely be put to death." The Old Testament only knew one penalty for breaking sabbath rest: death.

For example, if you built a fire on the sabbath, you would be put to death (Exodus 35:3). If you want to claim today, "I'm going to keep the sabbath like they did in the Old Testament," you're going to have a lot of trouble next Saturday. Don't start your car engine, for example, or you'll be starting a fire in every one of those cylinders. Be careful not to flick on a light switch, lest you start a fire in that incandescent bulb. And if it's cold next Saturday, don't turn your thermostat up and start a fire in your furnace. Do any of these things and you have committed a crime wor-thy of death, at least if you put yourself under the Old Testament sabbath covenant that was made between God and Israel.

But that was just the beginning. There are thirty-nine words in the Hebrew text of the Fourth Commandment. So the Jews added to the Word of God and found thirty-nine ways to break the sabbath. But they weren't content with that, so they took each of those ways and broke them down into thirty-nine divisions. When they finished, they had 1,521 ways to break the sabbath.

Nothing escaped their notice. If you got a tack in your sandal, better take it out on Friday night before sunset or you'll be carrying a burden and breaking the sabbath. If you got a flea on you, you'd better get him off before sunset on Friday. If not, and you try to kill him on Saturday, you are hunting on the sabbath day. You could put vinegar in your mouth and swallow it on the sabbath, because it was all right to eat. But don't hold the vinegar in your mouth very long if you have a toothache, for that would be to practice healing on the sabbath day. It got so bad that the Jews would not eat an egg that was laid on Saturday because that hen had worked on the sabbath day.

The sabbath was supposed to be a blessing to Israel. But they so contorted it that what was meant to be a blessing became a heavy burden. It was these minute sabbath laws that Jesus ignored, and for which He was hated by the Pharisees as a sabbath-breaker.

It didn't matter that Jesus was going around healing and doing works of mercy and love on the sabbath. He wasn't saluting their twisted version of God's covenant rest. You can see why Jesus told the scribes and Pharisees, "Thus have ye made the commandment of God of none effect by your tradition" (Matthew 15:6).

Calvary Rest

Here's the third rest, the one that applies to you and me. The third rest we find in the Bible is Calvary rest. This is the fulfillment of the sabbath for us, and this is how the Fourth Commandment applies to us in the church today.

The Old Testament sabbath, like all of the Old Testament ceremonies, was also a prophecy that pointed to something even more wonderful. The Bible says that the sabbath God gave to the covenant nation of Israel was a shadow that pointed toward the Lord Jesus Christ.

When did God rest? After His first creation. When did Jesus rest? After His new creation. The Bible says that if any man be in Christ—that's us—he is a new creation (2 Corinthians 5:17).

You see, Jesus came to do a work. He came to create a new race of people, a new creation. Jesus said, "I must work the works of him that sent me, while it is day" (John 9:4). Jesus did not come to earth to rest. He came to complete the work of redemption, and when He bowed

His head on the cross He said, "It is finished" (John 19:30). His work was done.

The Bible gives us this glorious picture of the resurrected Christ at rest: "But this man, after he had offered one sacrifice for sins for ever, sat down on the right hand of God" (Hebrews 10:12). Jesus did His work. It's finished, and now He is sitting down.

In the Old Testament temple, the priest had no place to sit because his work of offering sacrifices was never done. But Jesus "offered one sacrifice for sins for ever." His work of redemption is finished, and He is resting.

That means great blessing for you and me. The apostle Paul writes, "And you, being dead in your sins and the uncircumcision of your flesh, hath he quickened together with him [that is, with Jesus], having forgiven you all trespasses" (Colossians 2:13).

What does that mean? When Jesus rose from the grave, we rose with Him because we are forgiven of all our sins. Praise God! We were dead, and now we're alive. We were in sin, and now we are forgiven.

But there's more. Jesus also "blot[ted] out the handwriting of ordinances that was against us, which was contrary to us, and took it out of the way, nailing it to his cross" (verse 14).

This is tremendous because in Bible times if a man was judged guilty of a crime, the court clerk would record his crime. That document would then be nailed to the door of the man's prison cell, and he would not be released until his debt to society was paid. That paper was called a certificate of debt.

But look what Jesus did with the certificate of debt that was against us as criminals against heaven's King. He blotted it out. He tore it off the prison door and stamped it "Paid in full." That's what "It is finished" means in the Greek language—paid in full with the precious blood of the Lord Jesus Christ. He set the prisoners free. He released us from the prisonhouse of sin and invited us to share in His Calvary rest.

I hope you're getting a sense of the privilege that is ours when it comes to this matter of rest. God's creation rest has been disturbed. The rest of the Old Testament sabbath became an unbearable burden for the people who were supposed to enjoy it. But in Christ our rest is complete. Hallelujah!

Returning to Colossians 2, Paul has something wonderful to tell us based on Christ's redemption. First of all, notice in verse 15 that Jesus accomplished all of this in the face of Satan's fiercest opposition. Satan hounded Jesus to the cross. But Satan's seeming victory was his biggest defeat. Jesus destroyed him who had "the power of death" (Hebrews 2:14). Now look at verses 16-17 of Colossians 2:

> Let no man therefore judge you in meat, or in drink, or in respect of an holy-day, or of the new moon, or of the sabbath days [literally, "the sabbath"]: which are a shadow of things to come; but the body is of Christ.

What was the Old Testament sabbath? "A shadow of things to come," the shadow of which the reality was Jesus Christ. Nobody can rightfully say to you, "You started a fire on the sabbath day. You ought to be stoned. You took a sabbath day's journey and went too far. You ought to be punished." These things were the shadow. Don't let anybody judge you. That was the covenant sabbath, the covenant rest between God and Israel. It was only a shadow of things to come.

Have you ever seen a dog chasing the shadow of a bird flying overhead? That's an apt illustration of people who are still trying to keep the Old Testament covenant sabbath. They're chasing shadows, while the reality, "the body" of the whole matter, is passing them by. The reality is Jesus. The Old Testament covenant sabbath is only the shadow on the ground that points to the reality above.

The point is, don't miss Jesus. That's the reason Jesus could say in Matthew 11:28, "Come unto me, all ye that labor and are heavy laden, and I will give you rest."

What a glorious invitation. "I am your rest. I am now sitting at the right hand of the Father. My work is done. It is finished. Your sin-debt is paid in full." Can you see the joy of Jesus' finished work, providing rest for you?

THE LORD'S DAY

We celebrate the first day of the week as our day of rest and worship, not the seventh day. Why? Because Jesus burst asunder the bonds of death and came out of His grave on the first day of the week. Thus it is called "the Lord's day" in Revelation 1:10.

The Old Testament covenant rest is never called that. But the new creation, Calvary sabbath, is called the Lord's day. Let me give you eight brief, biblical reasons for celebrating the Lord's day:

1. We've already noted the first. Jesus rose from the dead on the first day of the week (Mark 16:9).

2. Jesus met with His disciples after His resurrection on the first day of the week. Compare John 20:19 and 26 and you'll see that Jesus appeared to the disciples on the day of His resurrection, "the first day of the week." He appeared again to them eight days later, counting each Sunday as one of the eight days.

3. The disciples were commissioned to preach the Gospel on the first day of the week—at that meeting on resurrection day (John 20:21).

4. The Holy Spirit was also imparted to the apostles on the first day of the week (John 20:22).

5. The church was born on the first day of the week, because the Day of Pentecost was on a Sunday (Acts 2:1).

6. The book of the Revelation was given on the first day of the week (Revelation 1:10).

7. The early church regularly met for worship on the first day of the week (Acts 20:7).

8. The church collected its offerings on the first day of the week as they came together (1 Corinthians 16:2).

Remember, Sunday is not the last day of your weekend; it is the first day of the week, and you start it right by being in the house of God. The disciples met together to break bread, preach the Word, observe the Lord's Supper, and collect their offerings on the first day of the week.

You cannot escape the weight of the biblical evidence. Our Lord has fulfilled the Old Testament sabbath. He has transformed it into Calvary rest. When Jesus uttered His triumphant, "It is finished," the work was done. We are now invited to enter into rest with Him.

The covenant sabbath speaks of the finished work of creation. The believer's Calvary rest speaks of the finished work of redemption. The first rest deals with natural life. Our rest with Christ deals with supernatural life.

The first sabbath rest dealt with life in Adam. Our sabbath rest deals with life in Christ. The first commemorated the work of God's hands. Ours commemorates the work of God's heart. The first was a display of God's power. Ours is a display of His grace. The first was given to Israel. The second was given to the church. The first was a day of law. Ours is a day of love.

Believe it, friend! Those who insist on keeping the Old Testament covenant rest are on the wrong side of Calvary. They're still chasing shadows. Jesus is saying, "Come unto me, and I will give you rest."

That brings up a question: if we're not under those laws of the Old Testament sabbath, how then do we keep the Lord's day? What are the regulations for keeping the first day of the week?

I cannot give you any rules, because the Bible does not give any. We've already seen that you cannot take the Old Testament rules concerning the sabbath and try to apply them today, because you'll get in trouble in an instant. You'll be breaking the sabbath every time you turn around.

But that doesn't mean we have jettisoned the Fourth Commandment and God's original intention to give us a day of holiness and rest. Let's consider how this applies to the church of the Lord Jesus Christ today.

Is the Lord's day a holy day? Absolutely. It's holy because it's His. But it's a day of love and not legalism. That usually raises questions like these: "Pastor, does that mean it's all right to watch television on Sunday? Is it all right to go to a ball game on Sunday? Can we eat out, read the newspaper, play softball, go boating, or go grocery shopping on Sunday?"

Those are good questions. The only thing wrong with them is that you asked the wrong man. It's not my day. It's the Lord's day. Ask Him. "Lord, how can I honor You on this day? How can I take this day and give You glory, reverence, and praise so at the end of the day I can say it was Your day?"

Someone will say, "Well, Adrian, every day's a holy day with me." That's true, but the Lord's day is extra-special. We're told to pray without ceasing, but Jesus also said that when you pray, enter into your closet. That's extra-special. We know that all of our possessions belong to God, but He also tells us to bring our offering to Him on the first day of the week. That's extra-special. When we bring our offering, it's a token that all we have belongs to God. And when we keep the Lord's day, it's a token that every day belongs to God.

I want to give you three principles to help you keep what I consider to be a wonderful Lord's day. The Lord's day is like calling "time out" in a ball game. It's a time out for God, a time we set aside for His use. So here are three basic principles that I believe will help make your home successful as you teach your children to keep the Lord's day. Here's how to make the rest day the best day.

A Holy Day

Make the Lord's day a holy day. Take time to be holy and to worship on the Lord's day.

We know the Bible commands New Testament Christians to come together for worship. Hebrews 10:25 says we are not to forsake the assembling of ourselves together. And we know that the day set aside for the church's worship is the first day of the week. So make family worship a priority on the Lord's day.

One of the best things a father can do for his family is to make church attendance a regular habit in his home. Little eyes are watching, Dad; little ears are listening. Make sure they see and hear the right things. "One generation shall praise thy works to another, and shall declare thy mighty acts" (Psalm 145:4). "The father to the children shall make known thy truth" (Isaiah 38:19).

Dad, make your worship on Sunday your highest priority—more important than your work on Monday. Don't give God excuses you wouldn't try on your boss. Imagine calling your employer one morning and saying, "I didn't come to work yesterday because we had unexpected company." Or, "You know, I was going to come to work, but I was just so tired, I slept in yesterday morning." Or how about this one? "I'm sorry I didn't come to work yesterday, but things have been pretty hectic around here, so the family decided we'd go to the beach." I don't think your boss would buy any of those reasons for missing work.

Do you know what you say to your children when you don't make church attendance a regular habit? You're saying it's nice, but it's not a necessity. But when you go to work every day, the kids know that's important. Teach your children what's really important.

When you get up and go to worship on the Lord's day, you're saying, "God is important to me. My church is important to me. My brothers and sisters in Christ are important to me." What a wonderful message to instill in your children's heart, because if all of this is important to you, it will be important to them.

How can you teach your children to love the Lord's day? Joyce and I raised four children who love the Lord, so we began to think back about ways we tried to make the Lord's day special for them. Here are some of the things we came up with:

Don't wait until Sunday to prepare for Sunday. Teach your children to anticipate the Lord's day by getting ready for Sunday on Saturday night. The Old Testament sabbath began at sunset on Friday. There is wisdom in that for us. Save your Saturday nights to get ready for the Lord's day. Get the shoes polished and the clothes laid out on Saturday night. Find your Sunday school lesson and go over it Saturday night. Get your offering out on Saturday night, and have it ready so your Sunday mornings won't be so frenetic.

Listen, it's often harder to get ready for Sunday school than it is for regular school. You have to prepare. And, fathers, help get the children ready. I heard about one woman who finally said to her husband, "Look, if you'll come in here and help get the kids ready, I'll go out and sit in the car and honk the horn." Touché!

Have a nice breakfast on Sunday morning. Take time for special prayer for the worship services and the Sunday school teachers and so forth. Joyce and I try to have breakfast together and pray for other pastors here in Memphis. Then we pray for the pastors across America and around the world.

Let your children enter into that time of prayer. Help them develop a prayer concern for their Sunday school teachers. You'll be surprised at the difference it will make in their attitudes. If your children are small, give them a special offering so that when they come to church, they are giving something. Older children need to learn to give out of their own earnings or allowance.

Be positive about church. Say a good word about the church in front of your children. Don't criticize the church in your children's presence. If you have a word of criticism, say it at the right time in the right spirit to the right person.

Bring your children to church. Encourage them to sing with you. Get them a Bible they can read. Help them take notes. Discuss the things of God in the house of God. Make church attendance a wonderful and happy thing. Take time to make the Lord's day a holy day.

A Healthy Day

Make the Lord's day a time to be healthy. You should not only worship on this day, but rest as well.

You may say, "Don't worry, Adrian, I don't need to teach my children how to rest. They already know how to do that."

That's not the kind of rest the Fourth Commandment is talking about. Going back to Exodus 20:9, let me remind you that the principle of sabbath rest is predicated on six days of labor. We need to teach our children how to work, because this Commandment not only tells us to rest—it tells us to work.

There was a young fellow who was used to having his dad just give him whatever he wanted. Well, his dad finally got tired of it, so one day when the boy wanted to go to a movie, he said, "Hey, Dad, can I have some money so I can hit the flick?"

His dad said, "No. You can flop the mop and swish the dish and spread the bed. But you can't hit the flick."

We need to teach our children industry. But we also need to teach them tranquillity. Take the Lord's day and rest. Slow down. Someone has said that if you're burning the candle at both ends, you're not as bright as you think you are.

You say, "I just can't get caught up. My ox keeps falling in the ditch, so to speak." Maybe you need to kill the ox or fill up the ditch. I'm not trying to give you a rule. I'm trying to give you a principle. Namely: you will do more work in six days if you learn to rest one day than you'll do in seven days without rest. In the same way, you'll have more money to spend with 90 percent and God as a partner than you'll have if you keep it all to yourself.

Make your Lord's day a day of rest. That's what He designed it to be. That's His will for you. A man who chops wood doesn't waste time when he sharpens his axe. You'll chop more wood if you'll learn to make the Lord's day a healthy day.

A Happy Day

I believe Sunday ought to be the happiest day of the week.

Why did the early church meet on Sunday? To celebrate the fact that Jesus came out of the grave on that day. After the resurrection of Jesus Christ, there's not a pessimistic or negative note in the New Testament. It's a celebration, a joy. Every Lord's day is Easter.

We get all happy about Easter. But we ought to come to church every Lord's day with the light of the noonday sun on our faces. Jesus is alive! He's risen! On the Lord's day we rejoice in His presence. This is the day that the Lord has made—a day of gladness, not of gloom; of love, not of legalism.

Let there be joy in your home on the Lord's day. Why not reinstitute the wonderful tradition of old-fashioned Sunday dinners where the family gets together to laugh, talk, and love. Take this day for music and books and conversation. Make the Lord's day the happiest day of the week, and your children will look back on these days with happy memories.

Let me leave you with this: remember the sabbath day not as a day of legalism that God gave to the Jews so long ago, but as a day of liberty—Jesus has set us free to love and serve Him!

What I have written in this chapter will mean absolutely nothing to you unless you understand the truth behind it. Jesus is your rest. I don't know your heart. So let me just say that if you have never come to Jesus, it's your move. You don't have to wait on Him. He's already invited you to come.

Sometimes they put on a tombstone, "Rest in peace." But there won't be any peace or rest until you find peace in the Lord Jesus. If you're tired of trying, why don't you start trusting? I promise you on the authority of God's Word that if you'll trust Jesus Christ, you'll find the rest we've been talking about. "Come unto me, all ye that labor and are heavy laden, and I will give you rest."

TURNING THE COMMANDMENTS INTO COMMITMENTS

0-6 Years

- Get things started right by taking your children to church.
- Do everything you can to make Sunday a happy day—have music playing when the kids wake up, sing on your way to church, etc.
- Explain why Dad and Mom take a day of rest.
- Start a special "Sunday time" for your kids on Sunday afternoon during which you all listen to the music they choose or read to them any book they choose.

7-12 Years

- Develop family traditions that make Sunday special—perhaps a special breakfast or a family treat after church.
- Teach your children how to be reverent without being rigid. Help them to see that worship is a heart issue, not an external one.
- Share with them the reasons Christians worship on the Lord's day and hold this day in special honor.
- Continue to help them develop the practice of regular giving on Sunday.

13+ Years

- On Saturday night, check with your teens to make sure the shirt or dress they plan to wear Sunday morning is ready, and so avoid panic or frantic digging in the clothes hamper the next morning.
- Speak well of the church in front of your children.
- Be available to help your children make decisions that honor God's day of rest and worship.
- Check regularly to see that your work and worship are balanced and providing a good example.

6

HAS THE NUCLEAR FAMILY BOMBED?

Nearly all that I know about God I learned first from my father.

—*Raymond I. Lindquist* [1]

Unless you have been hiding in a cave for the past few years, you probably remember the most famous verbal battle in recent American history: *Dan Quayle vs. Murphy Brown*.

Then Vice-president Quayle was speaking to the Commonwealth Club in San Francisco when he lit the fuse that set off the firestorm. He was talking about families, and in particular the problem of absentee fathers as it related to the rise in crime and the terrible disintegration of the home.

In the midst of that address, Quayle inserted this little paragraph that caused the media to come down on him like a junkyard dog:

> It doesn't help matters when prime-time TV has Murphy Brown—a character who supposedly epitomizes today's intelligent, highly paid professional woman—mocking the importance of fathers by bearing a child alone, and calling it just another "lifestyle choice." [2]

That's all Dan Quayle said. But what a howl those few words set off in the media. They called him antiquated, narrow-minded, idealistic. They made him look like a fundamentalist buffoon.

We'll talk about the values battle below, but what I want you to see first is the importance of Quayle's remarks. He is not alone in realizing that the disappearance of dads is destroying families, and that unless our nation undergoes some fundamental changes in the way we treat family life, we're headed for trouble.

Dan Quayle was not the first person to recognize the importance of both parents to healthy families. The Lord God Almighty established the primacy of parenthood for all time when He commanded us to "Honor thy father and thy mother: that thy days may be long upon the land which the LORD thy God giveth thee" (Exodus 20:12).

The Fifth Commandment is the first—and only—of God's Ten Commandments that comes with a direct promise attached to it. God created the nuclear family. But today we have to ask, has the nuclear family bombed? Is there hope for our families? I believe there is. You'll find it in the pages of God's Word.

But before we turn to God's prescription for successful families, I need to remind you that the battle has been joined for your family. The world is out to redefine the family today. Dan Quayle was treated with such scorn because he dared to run counter to the values Hollywood is trying to cram down our throats.

It always amazes me when evangelical Christians are accused of trying to cram their family values down other people's throats. Really? Who has redefined when life begins? It's not Christians. Who has changed the way Americans think about premarital sex? Don't look at us. Who is so eager to reshape our definition of family to include any and every grouping of people imaginable?

You know the answer as well as I do. The technicians of the "new" family aren't in the church but in the popular media, the universities, and other centers of thought and entertainment. You don't have to look any further than the United Nations Fourth World Conference on Women held during the late summer of 1995 in Beijing, China. In a letter written to friends of Focus on the Family in August 1995, Dr. James Dobson said this when discussing the "deconstruction of gender" that that conference hoped to accomplish:

The goal is to give members of the human family five genders from which to choose instead of two. When freed from traditional biases, a person can decide whether to be male, female, homosexual, lesbian, or transgendered. Some may want to try all five in time. Homosexuality is considered the moral equivalent of heterosexuality. For women, however, the preferred love relationship is lesbian in nature. In that way male oppressiveness can be negated. Artificial insemination is the ideal method of producing a pregnancy, and a lesbian partner should have the same parenting rights accorded historically to biological fathers.

The world is trying to remake the family in its image, and it's time God's people said, "Enough is enough." So let's begin our study of the Fifth Commandment by asking and answering this question: why did God give us families?

First of all, *God gave us families for living together*. Your family is intended to be a little part of the Garden of Eden that you carry with you. God established family life in the Garden, and sin didn't change that. Children still need families.

God also gave us families for learning. As I said before, the Ten Commandments were given primarily to the home, not to the school or the government or the business world. They apply there, but they're primarily for the home. We need to stop complaining that the Ten Commandments are not displayed on the classroom walls of our public schools if we ourselves don't display them and teach them in our homes.

Families are also for lasting. That's what the promise attached to this Commandment is all about. The Bible is not saying that every single child who obeys his parents will enjoy long life. But one thing is sure: a quick way to a shortened life is to disobey your parents. When the home begins to decay, it follows as surely as night follows day that the nation will begin to decay.

BECOMING WORTHY OF HONOR

I want to turn the Fifth Commandment around and think with you about being the kind of fathers and mothers their children can honor. Why? Because quite frankly I can't teach your children to honor you.

That's your responsibility. This book is not written primarily to the children. It's written to you as parents; so the best thing I can do in these few pages is to help you become a mom or dad who is worthy of honor.

Now it is true that whether a parent is worthy or not, there's a sense in which all children ought to honor their parents. But how much better it is when we live honorable lives before our children. Not perfect lives, but honorable lives.

Let's admit it. There has not been a perfect parent on this earth since Adam and Eve before the Fall. Don't ever get the idea that you have to be a perfect parent to live up to the Fifth Commandment. You're not a perfect parent, and your children are not perfect children.

You also cannot guarantee how your children will turn out. Some people have almost put themselves in an early grave because they've had a wayward child. They prayed, sacrificed, loved, and taught, and their child made bad choices anyway. Then somebody came along and laid Proverbs 22:6 on these hurting parents.

We are going to spend the final chapter of this book on this crucial verse and many other verses in Proverbs that relate to child-rearing, so I don't want to steal too much of that thunder here. But let me make some general observations.

If you try to turn all of the Bible proverbs into iron-clad promises, you'll lose your faith. That's what a lot of people have done with Proverbs 22:6. But think about it. There are proverbs that tell us how to be wealthy. Does that mean that everybody who follows those proverbs will automatically be wealthy? Of course not. Many godly people are not wealthy.

A proverb is a general principle that when generally applied brings a general result. It's a short sentence based on long experience. We use modern-day proverbs like, "Early to bed and early to rise will make you healthy, wealthy, and wise." Well, I suppose that's true, but you may also get hit by a truck!

I'm not trying to say the Bible is not to be taken seriously. It is. But you have to understand that God gave your child a will. He had two children of His own in the Garden of Eden, and they didn't do so hot.

Why? Because God gave them a will. That's the reason I believe you ought not to have goals for your children. I don't have goals for my children and grandchildren. I have desires for them, but I can't control what they do and become, and I wouldn't want to. But I do have goals for myself because I can control myself, by God's grace.

My desire is for godly children and grandchildren. My goal is to be a godly father and grandfather, worthy of their honor. Do I believe in the principle of Proverbs 22:6, that if I train my children in the way they should go, they will not depart from it? Absolutely! But I also know they have a will of their own.

What I'm trying to do is to relieve you from the burden of perfectionism that says if your child fails, it's your fault—it's because you did something wrong or didn't do something right. Let's turn it around. If your children's success depends upon your being a perfect parent, they will fail because nobody is perfect.

It's only by the grace of God that any of us survive parenthood. We enter this role totally inexperienced, and by the time we get the experience we need, we're unemployed. Thank God for grandchildren. Play it again!

So don't pretend to your children that you're perfect. They know you're not. What they want to know is, are you real? Are you genuine? If they know you're real, and they watch you handle your failures and problems, they will learn far more from that than they'll learn from any phony perfectionism.

HOW TO GAIN YOUR CHILDREN'S HONOR

So let's talk about living in such a way that our children can give us honor. I want to give you five simple and very achievable ways you can not only gain your children's honor, but prepare them to live successfully for the Lord and in turn become honor-worthy parents themselves.

By Loving Them

The first way you can become a father or mother worthy of being honored is by loving your children. Now in case you didn't know it, real parental love is not giving your children what they want, but what they need. That may seem like a truism, but it needs to be said because all of the values and principles you and I may take for granted are up for grabs today.

How do you love your child? Let me share with you a few ideas that

I've learned through my years of raising children and that I'm now using again with my grandchildren. I'm a bona fide grandfather. I've got the credentials and the scars to prove it.

One way to love your children is by *touching* them. I like the bumper sticker that says, "Kids need hugs, not drugs." That's a good one. Don't get the idea that you're not supposed to touch and hug your children, even your grown children.

What did the father of the prodigal son do when his son came home from the far country? He "fell on his neck, and kissed him" (Luke 15:20). This is a grown man with his grown son who had been living with the pigs! What a beautiful picture of fatherly love! Jesus told that story with approval. That's the way a father is supposed to love.

Did you know that frequent hugs are one good way to keep your children from growing up to be sexually impure? A girl who enjoys her father's hugs of affection is less likely to trade sexual intimacy for affection later. Hug your kids often. Hug them affectionately. Hug them supportively. Hug them tenderly. Hug them playfully, even when that teenaged boy says, "Aw, Mom" and tries to pull away. Inside, he still wants you to hug him, so just go ahead and do it. And, Dad, you hug your boy too.

Let your children see you hugging one another too. Joyce and I were locked in a tight embrace one day when our grandkids walked in on us in the kitchen. They just stood there, looked at us for a while, and then walked away. That's fine. They need to see us loving one another. They need to understand that to be huggable and lovable, they don't have to give sexual intimacy.

Charles Swindoll has said, "Many a young woman who opts for immoral sexual relationships does so because she can scarcely remember a time when her father so much as touched her. Unaffectionate dads, without wishing to do so, can trigger a daughter's promiscuity."[3]

All of this leads me to write with a great deal of passion: *Dad, don't hold back your affection.* Demonstrate your feelings of love to both sons and daughters, and don't stop once they reach adolescence. They long for your affirmation and appreciation. They will love you for it. More importantly, they will emulate your example when God gives them their own families. Love your children by touching them.

You can also love your kids by *blessing* them. The Bible teaches that we parents have an awesome weapon called a blessing. We can bless our kids in such an incredible way. There are few things in life that will give your children more peace and confidence than the gift of your blessing. My father blessed me, and I praise God for it.

Your kids need strokes, not just pokes. They need you to say, "In the name of Jesus, my child, I bless you." Can you imagine what it does for a child when his dad sweeps him up in his arms and says, "Billy, you are special to God"? He'll never forget it.

Older children need your blessing in a different way. They need to know that you believe in them and have high hopes for their future. They need to know that as they dream and hope and plan, they have your blessing to go for it, to be all that God wants them to be.

What's the opposite of the blessing? The father who says, "Son, I always wanted to be a doctor, but I never had that opportunity. So you're going to be a doctor." The son's response may be, "But, Dad, I don't want to be a doctor." "Son, you're going to be a doctor."

You also bless your children when you take their joys and sorrows seriously. Little children hurt. Don't laugh at their pain when the doll is broken or the pet lizard dies or the turtle does a bottoms-up and floats to the top. Children's pain in their world is just as real as your pain in your world.

We've had several funerals for dogs in our family. I mean the full thing, with flowers and everything. We buried that hound and held hands, and it was real to the children. Sometimes it's real to us adults too, but we don't like to admit it.

We need to bless and comfort our children, to pick them up and say, "I understand, and I hope it'll feel better later" and kiss away those tears. I know what it is to hold a grown child in my arms when her heart was broken and my heart was broken and both of us cried like babies.

Let me tell you another way to love your children—by *listening* to them. We adults think we listen, but all too often the kids barely get a full sentence out of their mouths before we jump in with our advice.

One of the finest forms of communication is saying nothing. If you have a teenager, you know you have to be ready to listen at any hour of the day or night. About 11 P.M. one night, when you're so sleepy you can't wait to go to bed, that teen will start talking. You'd better decide now that you'll pay the price to listen, especially if your teen is having a problem in his or her social life or struggling with their feelings about themselves. Sit down and listen, and you'll communicate your love without having to say a word.

Love your children steadfastly, consistently. They need to know that Mom and Dad love them, no matter what. Give your kids time to go through these different stages. We live in an age where we want everything, and we want it *now*. But you can't rush children through childhood. Give your kids time to grow up. Be consistent.

Finally, love your children with your *prayers*. Pray for them, pray for them again, and then pray for them some more. It's long been a morning practice in our home for Joyce and me to hold hands and bring our children and grandchildren to the Lord by name. The most loving thing you can do is to carry your children to the throne of grace in prayer.

By Lifting Them

A second way to gain your children's honor is by lifting them—building them up—through wise encouragement.

Colossians 3:21 is a key verse here: "Fathers, provoke not your children to anger, lest they be discouraged." Here's the principle: wise encouragement is better than lavish praise. You need to learn the difference between praise and encouragement, because children need encouragement more than they need praise.

Not long ago I bought Joyce a hanging basket of impatiens plants. But I went by one morning and they were just drooping all over the place. I thought they'd never come back, but I sprinkled them anyway. The transformation was amazing.

Children are like that. They need encouragement the way a plant needs water—over and over again, dose after dose, day after day. When you catch them doing something right, let them know through your encouragement that you believe in them. Let your speech affirm them.

What is the difference between encouragement and praise? Let's assume your child brings home straight A's. Praise says, "Oh, that's wonderful. You're brilliant. You're a hard worker. Daddy is so proud of you because you got straight A's." Or if you're one of those mothers who needs a riding vacuum to get through your child's room, you'll be tempted to lavish praise on him or her—"Mom's proud of you because you cleaned your room. I can see the rug now." But what that says to the child is, "I get approval when I do well. Approval is something I can earn. When I do the right things, my parents approve. So I'll just make sure I do well so they won't disapprove of me, and my self-image won't go down the tubes."

Praise says, "Great! You cleaned up your room." In contrast, encouragement says, "It's great that your room got cleaned up. I really appreciate your effort." There's a difference between those two messages. Encouragement focuses primarily on the child doing the achieving, not on the achievement itself. It says, "Thank you. I'm so grateful for you."

I'm not saying there's anything wrong with praise. But I do believe encouragement is twice as strong as praise because it shines the spotlight where it needs to be. You may need to think about this one for a while, but I hope you'll see the power of lifting your children through encouragement.

By Limiting Them

A third way to become the kind of parents children can honor is by setting healthy limits for them.

It takes firm restrictions to set children free. It is your responsibility to liberate your kids by limiting them. In 1 Samuel 3:13 God said this about the priest Eli: "I have told him that I will judge his house for ever for the iniquity which he knoweth; because his sons made themselves vile, and he restrained them not."

Eli didn't set any limits for his boys, and it cost all of them dearly. Your child needs to have limits. When God put Adam and Eve in the Garden, He gave them all they needed, but He also gave them some limits. There was one thing they could not do. Even though they did it anyway, God's example of setting limits is a positive one.

I say this because of a fact you already know if you're a parent: when you give your children limits, they will test those limits over and over again. Children push against their parents' restrictions to see if they will move—and if they do move, that child will lose his sense of security.

Remember, our limits have to be drawn in love. But if you will set firm limits, and if your children know you love them, when they push against the rules and those rules don't move, they have security.

A failure to place limitations on a child communicates not freedom to that child, but rejection. We all inwardly desire limits. If you don't conquer your child's will, somebody else will.

Society in general looks upon rule-setting as something bad, but it's one of the most valuable things a parent can do. There's something wrong with many of the young people in our evangelical churches today. As we saw back in Chapter Two, they can't tell right from wrong. What a job Satan is doing on the next generation. We need to ask the age-old question, "If the foundations be destroyed, what can the righteous do?" (Psalm 11:3). If our children don't learn to live within limits now, when will they?

A few years ago Ted Koppel of ABC News helped to put things in perspective during his address to the graduating class at Duke University. Here is a portion of what he said:

> In the place of truth we have discovered facts; for moral absolutes, we have substituted moral ambiguity. We now communicate with everyone and say absolutely nothing. We have reconstructed the Tower of Babel and it is a television antenna, a thousand voices producing a daily parody of democracy in which everyone's opinion is afforded equal weight regardless of substance or merit. Indeed, it can even be argued that opinions of real weight tend to sink with barely a trace in television's ocean of banalities. . . . What Moses brought down from Mount Sinai were not the Ten Suggestions; they are Commandments. Are, not were. The sheer beauty of the Commandments is that they codify in a handful of words acceptable human behavior, not just for then or now, but for all time.[4]

Our society is being systematically seduced away from the idea that life has any limits, that there is any such thing as moral absolutes. One of Hollywood's top producers of situation comedies is reported to have said that it was his sincere conviction that for any television script to be commercially successful, it had to violate at least three of the Ten Commandments.

The whole point of a sitcom is to cause you to laugh at something.

And when you laugh at something, you don't take it seriously anymore. If the devil can get you laughing at someone else's transgression of the Ten Commandments, you won't take your own transgression that seriously. It will be funny. So we have a generation that's laughing its way into hell.

This is the reason you as parents need to set limits. Don't be afraid to tell your children that MTV, for example, is out of bounds, or that "Hell's Box Office," HBO, is not coming into your home. You are foolish if you think you or your children can watch immoral programming and not be affected. "Can a man take fire in his bosom, and his clothes not be burned?" (Proverbs 6:27). Set loving but firm limits.

By Leading Them

How can you be an honorable parent? By leading your children. By showing them how to do right rather than just telling them how to do right.

I want to go back to Proverbs 22:6 briefly and pick up on the key word in that verse: "train." We are to *train* our children in the way they should go. To teach without training is to fail in the task.

Can anybody learn to play football by reading books? No. A player who goes to football training camp doesn't spend his time in the library. A man who wants to train his hunting dogs takes them out in the woods. It's amazing. We train our dogs and don't train our kids. Then we tie up the dogs at night and let the kids run wild.

What do you want your children to be? I don't mean the profession you hope they'll choose. I'm talking about the kind of character you want them to develop and display. You've got to lead them in developing character. Show them by example what a man or woman of character looks like.

I thank the Lord that in a few places school administrators and teachers are starting to take notice of and implement character education. Maybe it will temper some of our undue emphasis on sports, grades, physical health, popularity, and ability.

Look at this list for a moment: contentment, courage, courtesy, discernment, fairness, friendliness, generosity, gentleness, helpfulness, honesty, humility, kindness, obedience, orderliness, patience, persistence, self-control, tactfulness, thankfulness, thriftiness, wisdom.

Who is teaching these qualities of character? Mom and Dad, it needs to be you. Learn to compliment character more than talent.

Let me give you a wonderful example of what it means to lead your children as a parent who wants to be honorable. I know this family, and I can vouch for the Christian character of both the parents and the children.

It seems that one of the boys lipped off to his mother one day. Now I don't know about your home, but in the Rogers home showing disrespect to Mama was not tolerated. It wasn't tolerated in this home either, because this boy's father said to him, "Son, I want to tell you something. When you lipped off to your mother, you sinned against God. God says you are to honor her, and you're going to have to answer to Him for that.

"Not only that, but you sinned against your mother. She went down into the valley of the shadow of death to bring you to life. How ungrateful you've been to speak to your mother that way, and you're going to have to answer to your mother for that."

And then this godly dad said, "I want to tell you something else. Not only is she your mother—she's my wife. And you're not going to talk that way to my wife. Now you not only have God and your mother to deal with, you've got me to deal with because you have shown disrespect to my wife."

I think that's one of the greatest training exercises I have ever heard of in my life. That's the kind of teaching, the kind of leading, I'm talking about. What a powerful impression a lesson like that would have on a young person.

By Laughing with Them

Do you want to be an honorable parent? Lighten up. Learn how to laugh. Make your home a place of joy and laughter. You need to learn how to laugh because serious situations often call for a lot of laughter.

Human beings are the only creatures of God who can laugh, weep, and blush. Our emotions are part of what it means to be made in God's image. As part of that, laughter is God's gift to us. Jesus said, "Blessed are ye that weep now: for ye shall laugh" (Luke 6:21). He is saying that laughter is a blessing. The poet Thackeray said laughter is like sunshine in the house. Let your kids see you laugh at yourself, at your mistakes.

Back in 1953, Eddie Fisher sang a song entitled "Oh, My Papa." It was a touching song about a man's remembrances of his father. The father was "so gentle and so lovable." He was "so funny and adorable, always the clown, so funny in his way." Then the song concluded, "O my papa, to me he was so wonderful. Deep in my heart, I miss him so today."

Everybody was singing that song and loving it, whether their dad was lovable and a funny clown or not. That's the kind of dad they wanted. I hope your house is filled with fun. Let your children bring their friends home. Let them raid the refrigerator. Let them mash down the couch a little bit. Don't worry so much about a few fingerprints on the wall. Thank God for them. You'll have plenty of time in your retirement years to repaint the walls!

Make your home the happiest place on the block, and your children will rise up and bless you for it. Let your house ring with laughter. Let your children see you laugh in times of trouble, because it means that God is over it all.

I remember one occasion when our children were young. We got in the car to go somewhere one day, and my son David, sitting in the backseat, had already put his window down. So when I turned on the air conditioning I said, "Son, put your window up." He hit the button to put the power window up, and we took off.

But a short while later I heard the sound of wind rushing through the car. I looked around, and David's window was down again. I said, "Son, put that window back up."

He obeyed, but soon I heard the wind roaring again. David had put his window down once more. By this time I was peeved, to put it spiritually. I said, "David, put that window up, and leave it up or there's going to be serious trouble. Do you understand?"

It got very quiet and tense in the car. "Yes, sir," he said, and the window went up.

Just then a sudden fit of mischievousness came over me. I reached over to the control panel on my door and quietly pushed the button to lower the window on David's side. Joyce turned around and said, "David!" as if it were the end of the world. But then she and David both realized what had happened, and we all had a big laugh that defused a tense situation. Laughter is good medicine.

HALL OF FAME PARENTS

In 1993 workers doing some moving and remodeling at the Baseball Hall of Fame in Cooperstown, New York, discovered something rather unusual. As they were moving a display cabinet, they found an old photograph tucked behind the case. It was a photo of a stocky, friendly-looking man in a baseball uniform with the words "Sinclair Oil" on the shirt.

Stapled to the picture was a note in a man's scrawl that said, "You were never too tired to play ball. On your days off, you helped build the Little League field. You always came to watch me play. You were a Hall of Fame dad. I wish I could share this moment with you."

No one knew how the picture got there or the identity of the dad in the photo. A national sports magazine picked up the touching story, and a man came forward to say that he had tucked the picture and the note behind the display case during a visit to the Hall of Fame.

It seems the ballplayer in the photo was this man's late father. Just like the note said, this man was proud of his dad and believed he deserved to receive special recognition. So he decided to honor his father by holding his own little ceremony to induct his dad into the Hall of Fame.

That's wonderful! What this man was saying was, "Dad, you deserve a place alongside the best ballplayers. You were a Hall of Fame father."

I want to be in that Hall of Fame, don't you? Let's be the kind of fathers and mothers who make it a joy and a delight for our children to obey God's command, "Honor thy father and thy mother."

TURNING THE COMMANDMENTS INTO COMMITMENTS

0-6 Years

- Very early on, establish a rule of absolute respect for Mother.
- Show your children that Dad and Mom are called to be obedient to their Heavenly Father.
- Honor your mate in your children's presence every chance you get.
- Help your children honor your mate on his or her special day (birthday, Mother's Day, Father's Day) by drawing a picture or making a card that expresses the child's love.

7-12 Years

- Explain to your children the ways you are honoring your parents (love, respect, prayer, seeking their counsel, perhaps even physical care).

- Deal swiftly with disrespect and sass.

- Determine to avoid using even humorous or gentle put-downs of your mate.

13+ Years

- Encourage your children's friends to honor their parents.

- Be ready to admit it when you blow it, then go on from there.

- Remind your children of the promise attached to this Commandment.

- Remind them that they will want their children to honor them someday.

7

FAMILIES THAT CHOOSE LIFE

*No previous age has equalled our horror of killing; but
then, no previous age ever killed so much!*

—*R. Kent Hughes* [1]

Life is God's wonderful gift to us. Since He is the author of life, He also gets to set the rules by which it is to be lived. I believe God established the sanctity of human life the moment He created Adam and Eve in His image. Long before the Sixth Commandment was ever given, we see God holding the first murderer, Cain, fully accountable for his crime (Genesis 4:8-12).

Later, after the Flood, God gave this command to Noah: "Whoso sheddeth man's blood, by man shall his blood be shed: for in the image of God made he man" (Genesis 9:6). This verse is very instructive to us because it answers the two most common misunderstandings and misapplications of the Sixth Commandment. Let me show you what I mean.

A SPECIFIC COMMANDMENT

Genesis 9:6 clearly prohibits murder. That's important because this is also the intent of the Sixth Commandment, "Thou shalt not kill" (Exodus 20:13). This is a very specific command, not just a general prohibition against all forms of life-taking. The word translated "kill" is actually a rather rare Hebrew word that means "murder."

In fact, the *New International Version* so translates this word in Exodus 20:13—"You shall not murder." So, for instance, those who break into laboratories to set experimental mice or rats free or smash the lobster tank at a restaurant to free the lobster on the premise "Thou shalt not kill" are about as far off the mark as they can get. This Commandment has absolutely nothing to do with this extreme animal rights nonsense. It is a prohibition against the willful taking of human life.

More serious is the argument that the Sixth Commandment forbids capital punishment. Those who hold this position argue that the death penalty is merely state-sanctioned murder that only multiplies the violence.

That argument finds no support in Scripture. The very fact that human life is sanctified in God's sight makes the deliberate taking of a life in murder the most heinous act possible. In fact, the Bible is very clear and very specific about the penalty for violating this Commandment.

Genesis 9:6 spells out for all generations the penalty for murder: the forfeiture of the murderer's own life. Later God made capital punishment a permanent part of Israel's law code. In the very next chapter after the giving of the Ten Commandments, Moses records God's punishment for deliberate, premeditated murder. It is death at the hands of the duly appointed authorities (Exodus 21:12, 14).

The purpose of this chapter is not to debate capital punishment. But it's important that you understand God's intent behind His Commandments, because our society is moving further and further away from the bedrock biblical teaching of the sanctity of human life.

You need to teach your children the value of this thing called life and the seriousness of taking another life. But what I want to develop for you in the remainder of this chapter is the positive side of the Sixth Commandment, which I have expressed in the chapter title. I want to help you teach your children to choose life.

Remember our basic premise that for every negative command God gives, there is a positive implied. So I say we ought to enjoy life, and we ought to choose life.

THE GREAT LIFE-GIVER

Jesus is the great Life-giver. Satan is the great life-destroyer. The Lord Jesus said so Himself in John 10:10, the key verse in the New Testament that helps us to understand the Sixth Commandment: "The thief cometh not, but for to steal, and to kill, and to destroy: I am come that they might have life, and that they might have it more abundantly."

When Jesus talks about the thief here, He's talking about Satan. "Thief" is Jesus' name for Satan. As a thief, Satan's only purpose is to destroy our lives. But Jesus has come to give us life. So as we talk about helping your family choose life, I want you to think with me about the Lord Jesus Christ as the great Life-giver who gives us three kinds of life.

Physical Life

Jesus has given us physical life. The very fact that you are able to read this book with eyes that see and a heart that beats and ears that are able to receive sound is because Jesus has given you life. The Bible says that all things were made by Him (John 1:3; Colossians 1:16), and that includes us.

And how did He make you? Genesis 2:7 says it so clearly: "The LORD God formed man of the dust of the ground, and breathed into his nostrils the breath of life; and man became a living soul." Here is a truth you need to teach over and over again to your children, because they're not going to get it in the public schools.

What they are going to get instead is the "monkey mythology" of evolution that doesn't explain anything. There is no evolutionist on earth who has enough degrees after his name to explain the origin of life. Evolution falls apart completely at this point, even if it didn't fall apart at every other point.

To say that life came about through spontaneous generation in some primordial soup is laughable, especially since evolution can't even account for the origin of the soup. There is another agenda at work here, a blatant denial of the truth of God's creation.

Dr. George Wald, a Nobel prize winner in science, once said this about the origin of life:

> When it comes to the origin of life on this earth, there are only two possibilities: creation or spontaneous generation. There is no third way. Spontaneous generation, was disproved 100 years ago, but that leads us only to one other conclusion: that of supernatural creation.[2]

So far so good, wouldn't you agree? But Dr. Wald doesn't stop there. He continues:

> We cannot accept that [i.e., the conclusion that life arose as a supernatural creative act of God] on philosophical grounds; therefore, we choose to believe the impossible: that life arose spontaneously by chance.[3]

This is why I say that evolution is not science. It is a bias against Almighty God. And because it is the dominant theory of origins in our culture and in our educational system, we need to teach our children that Jesus Christ is the author of physical life.

Spiritual Life

Jesus also gives us spiritual life. He said, "I am the way, the truth, and the life; no man cometh unto the Father, but by me" (John 14:6).

When Jesus said "I am the way," He was saying, "Without Me there is no going." When He said, "I am the truth," He was saying, "Without Me there is no knowing." When He said, "I am the life," He was saying, "Without Me there is no growing."

Christians are not just nice people who are trying to do better. They are not just those who have accepted some doctrinal creed or code of conduct. They are new creatures, having been supernaturally regenerated and transformed by Jesus Christ, who sends His Spirit into their hearts and gives them supernatural life.

Eternal Life

This same Jesus who gives us physical and spiritual life also gives us eternal life. In John 10:27-28 Jesus says this concerning those who believe in Him: "My sheep hear my voice, and I know them, and they follow me: and I give unto them eternal life; and they shall never perish." Jesus is the author of never-ending life.

Eternal life speaks of the quality of life as well as the quantity of life. Jesus adds years to the life and life to the years.

A little boy went to the pet store to buy a puppy. There were a lot of puppies, but one was sitting over in the corner wagging his tail. The little fellow noticed this particular puppy and said, "I want the one with the happy ending."

That's what I want. I want the life that has the happy ending. I want eternal life—life that never ends. Only Jesus can give this kind of life. So if your family would choose life that is life indeed, teach your children to choose Jesus.

THE LIFE-DESTROYER

If Jesus is the great Life-giver, as we saw in John 10:10, then Satan is the thief who comes to steal, kill, and destroy. He is the sinister minister of destruction. In John 8:44 Jesus was speaking to the Pharisees, and He told them, "Ye are of your father the devil, and the lusts of your father ye will do: he was a murderer from the beginning."

Since Satan is a murderer and the Sixth Commandment says, "Thou shalt not kill," this is another way of saying that we must reject Satan. We must choose life. Satan wants to bring death into your family. He wants to bring death to youth, death to purity, death to joy, death to happiness. He wants to bring physical death, spiritual death, and eternal death. He wants to make your life not abundant, but miserable.

Someone wrote these words: "A crust of bread and a corner to sleep in, a minute to smile, and an hour to weep in, a pint of joy, and a peck of trouble, and never a laugh, but the moan comes double, and this is life." Not if you know the Lord Jesus.

Someone has discovered that the word *evil* spelled backwards is *live*. The word *devil* spelled backwards is *lived*. Satan is antithetical to everything that spells life. Why does Satan hate life? Because he hates man. And why does he hate man? Because man is made in the image of God, and Satan hates God. But he cannot get at God, so he tries to get at you and your family instead.

Music has always been one of Satan's most effective weapons. So many modern rock groups are inspired and controlled by Satan. There's no other explanation for the names chosen for groups such as The

Grateful Dead, Annihilator, Atrocity, Carnivore, Coroner, The Damned, Dark Angel, Sluts from Hell, Atheist, Autopsy, Megadeath, Morbid Angel, Obituary, Death Angel, Destruction, Entombed, Legion of Death, Massacre, Napalm Death, Poison, Devastation, Guillotine, Malice, Violence, The Zombies, Oblivion, Slaughter, Suicidal Tendencies, Venom, Slayer, Thrasher, or Ultimate Revenge.

Such a fascination with death comes from the very pit of hell, but this is the kind of music that is being drummed into our young people's minds. Thousands of people of various ages flock to hear The Grateful Dead. I want to tell you, I'm grateful for life in the Lord Jesus Christ!

Satan is a thief and a murderer, and his method is deception. He wants to deceive, then to destroy, and then to damn. Sin thrills, and then it kills. Sin fascinates, and then it assassinates. Let's learn how to protect ourselves and our families against Satan, the destroyer of life.

PROTECTING LIFE

When the children of Israel were facing their inheritance, the Promised Land, Moses called them together and gave them this word in Deuteronomy 30:15-20:

> See, I have set before thee this day life and good, and death and evil; in that I command thee this day to love the LORD thy God, to walk in his ways, and to keep his commandments, and his statutes, and his judgments, that thou mayest live and multiply: and the LORD thy God shall bless thee in the land whither thou goest to possess it. But if thine heart turn away, so that thou wilt not hear, but shalt be drawn away, and worship other gods, and serve them; I denounce unto you this day, that ye shall surely perish, and that ye shall not prolong your days upon the land, whither thou passest over Jordan to go to possess it. I call heaven and earth to record this day against you, that I have set before you life and death, blessing and cursing: therefore choose life, that both thou and thy seed may live: that thou mayest love the LORD thy God, and that thou mayest obey his voice, and that thou mayest cleave unto him: for he is thy life, and the length of thy days: that thou mayest dwell in the land which the LORD sware unto thy fathers, to Abraham, to Isaac, and to Jacob, to give them.

What a great statement. The Lord is our life. It's not that He only gives life. He *is* life.

We're talking about helping our children choose life instead of death. Dad, it is primarily your job to protect that life. In Deuteronomy 22:8 God said, "When thou buildest a new house, then thou shalt make a battlement for thy roof, that thou bring not blood upon thine house, if any man fall from thence."

The father was to build a wall around the roof of his house. We would call it today a parapet or a rampart. It was designed to keep someone from falling off the roof. But if someone did fall, the father would not be held guilty if he had built a wall to protect the lives of those in the home. God said it is the father's responsibility to protect his family from death. If he didn't, he would be guilty of their blood, should one fall.

Having said all of that by way of background, let's see what fathers— and mothers too—are to do to protect life.

Intentional Murder

The family is meant to protect physical life. From what? First of all, from intentional killing, the crime of homicide, just as the Sixth Commandment says. The home was meant to be a place of safety. But many homes are so violent today that the young people in them are afraid to be at home, so they hang out on the streets.

We are a bloody and murderous society. The terrible bombing in Oklahoma City has only served to underscore that. True Christians are against killing. Genuine Christians believe in life. The blood of those who have been murdered in our streets cries out from the ground. And one day the God who said, "Thou shalt not kill" will judge all murderers.

Suicide

The family is also designed to protect its members from the crime of suicide. As I've been studying the home, I've been alarmed at the rate of teenage suicide. What a grievous thing it is for anybody to take his or her own life, especially a child or youth whose life Satan has succeeded in destroying.

Dad and Mom, help your children to understand that our lives are not our own to do with as we please. Our lives belong to God because He is the giver of life. Teach your kids that we should never take into our own hands matters that only God is wise enough, strong enough, and good enough to handle.

Could a Christian commit suicide in a moment of deep despondency or mental derangement? Yes, it happens; but it is never the answer of which God approves. Your children must see how hurtful and how shameful it will be when a person faces the Savior after taking his life, besides the shame and sorrow left behind for the family to bear.

Parents, teach your children the great truth that Jesus will give us grace to face whatever comes our way. Help them hide this verse in their hearts: "There hath no temptation taken you but such as is common to man: but God is faithful, who will not suffer you to be tempted above that ye are able; but will with the temptation also make a way to escape, that ye may be able to bear it" (1 Corinthians 10:13).

Abortion

A third way that our families need to protect life is by protecting the unborn from the crime of abortion. In America today, the lives of some 4,000 unborn babies a day are being snuffed out—and it's all legal. When the Supreme Court issued its infamous decision legalizing abortion in 1973, the Court ruled that every woman in the United States had as much right to an abortion as she did to any other "minor surgery."

What a deplorable way to classify the deaths of unborn children. Something is very wrong in America when we protect spotted owls and whales and snail darters and bald eagles, but have made a mother's womb the most dangerous place a baby can be.

The real issue, of course, is when life begins. Jeremiah 1:5 answers that if you're a Bible believer. God said to the prophet Jeremiah, "Before I formed thee in the belly I knew thee; and before thou camest forth out of the womb I sanctified thee, and I ordained thee a prophet unto the nations."

If you want your children to grow up to be people who choose and hallow life and in so doing obey the Sixth Commandment, you can't do any better than to teach them to choose and protect life while it is in the womb. That baby in the mother's womb is a separate life, with every component of life in it. Nothing new will develop. All he or she does at birth is pass on down through the birth canal.

If we do not protect life now, someday God will visit our sin upon our own heads. Someone has pointed out that the children this generation of adults has tried to abort may someday be the generation that approves and carries out our forced euthanasia!

Not too long ago I read an example of how far off the mark we have gotten when it comes to protecting human life versus other forms of life. It was an almost unbelievable story in the newspaper about an elderly man in New Jersey.

It seems that a rat was eating the tomatoes in this man's garden, so he set a trap and caught the rat. But the rat was trying to get out of the trap, so the man took a broomstick, wrapped it in newspaper, and beat that rat to death.

Well, that should have been the end of it, but the local Humane Society's executive director jumped to the defense of the rat. He had a summons issued for this elderly gardener's arrest for cruelty. The man faced a possible fine of $1,250 and six months in jail for killing the rat.

When the story got out and the executive director of the Humane Society found out that people were laughing at him all over America, he explained his charge by saying that the fact that the animal was killed was not the problem. The arrest summons was issued because the rat was trapped and could not escape and so had to suffer mutilation and a horrible death.

When I read that, I thought about little babies trapped in their mothers' wombs, suffering mutilation and a horrible death. Yet here's a man who wants to arrest someone for killing a rat who's been eating his tomatoes.

Dr. Landrun Shettles, a pioneer in the field of sperm biology, said this about abortion: "I oppose abortion. I do so because I accept what is biologically manifest. My position is scientific, pragmatic, and humanitarian."[4] As Christians, we go a step further. We oppose abortion because the Bible teaches that it is murder!

If the Sixth Commandment means anything, it means we must protect the unborn against the heinous sin of abortion.

Cruelty

We need to protect our family's social life because murder is not the only way to kill someone and transgress the Commandment of God. Cruelty too is a way of killing people. Some children have put wrinkles in their parents' brows and sent them to an early grave by their heartlessness. Some husbands have sent their wives to a premature death after years of cruelty. Cruelty may take years to kill its victim, but it's very effective.

The Chinese used to have an ancient form of torture and execution called the water torture. They would strap a man into a chair, put over his head a huge reservoir of water, and let the water drip onto his head as long as it took until finally his whole nervous system would explode and the man's life would end in horrible death. Some people are killing others in similar ways.

Death-dealing Businesses

Another reason we need to be families that choose and protect life is because of those who are engaged in corrupt and death-dealing businesses. I would never be in the whiskey business, not because of financial matters, but because of the Sixth Commandment that prohibits killing. The liquor industry has the curse of God upon it. Whiskey is brewed with tears and thickened with blood and flavored with death.

The prophet Habakkuk wrote, "Woe to him that buildeth a town with blood, and establisheth a city by iniquity!" (2:12). He also warned, "Woe unto him that giveth his neighbor drink, that puttest thy bottle to him, and makest him drunken" (2:15). People say alcohol is good for business. But God says if you build a civilization on it, you are inviting His judgment.

Robert McNamara, the Secretary of Defense during the Vietnam War, recently came out with a book that said Vietnam was a mistake and that the people in the White House knew it. But did you know that six times as many Americans lost their lives due to alcohol during that same period as were lost in the Vietnam War?

When is somebody going to say we made a mistake about alcohol? Nobody is going to say it. Yet every twenty-two minutes somebody is killed in an alcohol-related car accident. Every sixty seconds someone is maimed. We have four million teenage alcoholics in America today.

I agree with the person who said alcohol has many defenders, but it has no defense. It has turned our highways into slaughter alleys and our homes into prisons of despair. We fathers need to build a wall around the roof of our homes to keep our children from falling into this or other sin.

Dad, take your son or daughter to the hospital emergency room some Saturday night and let them see the carnage of a wreck caused by a drunken diver. Take them to the local rescue mission to meet the men and women whose lives have been ruined by alcohol. Help your children choose life.

Anger and Hatred

Here's where all of us need to pay close attention. We need to protect our personal and family spiritual life.

You may say, "Adrian, I'm not in the liquor business. I'm not an abortionist. I'm not a thief or a drug pusher. I don't listen to those rock bands that glorify Satan and death."

That's wonderful. But now let's talk about the life of the spirit, the things that fill our hearts. Our Lord said that we can transgress the spirit of the Sixth Commandment if we allow anger and hatred in our hearts against a brother or sister. "Whosoever hateth his brother is a murderer: and ye know that no murderer hath eternal life abiding in him" (1 John 3:15).

Do you hate somebody? Is your heart a headquarters for malice? I believe in salvation by grace, but according to John you cannot possess salvation and harbor hatred for your brother, whether it's racial, religious, or revengeful hate. Make your home a place of love, forgiveness, and happiness, not a refuge for bitterness. You'll be obeying God, and you'll help your children see the value of choosing spiritual life.

Protecting Eternal Life

But the best thing you as a father or mother can do to protect your family's eternal life is to lead your children to a saving knowledge of Jesus Christ.

I have four children on this earth and a little boy in heaven. My children are a long way from perfect, but they all love God. When my son, Steve, was a teenager, I didn't see the beauty of Jesus in his life, although he had made a profession of faith in Christ. I was concerned, so I asked Steve to take a ride with me one day.

We drove out to the woods, and I asked Steve to take a walk with me.

As we were walking, I said to him, "Son, I have got to know for sure that you know Jesus." And we talked about it.

I didn't try to put a stranglehold on Steve. I just wanted to know that he knew Jesus. And out there in the woods we knelt and prayed. He assured me, "Dad, I love Jesus." And he's showing it now through his life. He's a real man of God.

Another time I prayed, "Lord, if any of my children are not saved, please bring them to Yourself. Lord, I don't want to go to heaven without all my children."

I didn't say anything to my wife, Joyce, or to the children about the prayer of my heart. But the next Sunday when I gave the invitation, my oldest daughter, Gayle, came forward and said, "Daddy, I don't believe I've ever truly been saved. I want to be saved now." She gave her heart to Jesus that day, and I believe it was directly related to my prayer.

Dear Christian parent, help your family choose life. Dad, you've got to build a wall around the roof of your house lest your children fall off. Determine that you will not go to heaven without taking all of your children with you. Bring them to Jesus, the great Life-giver. Satan deals in death, but Jesus has come that we might have abundant and eternal life.

Turning the Commandments into Commitments

0-6 Years

- Pray for your children's safety (Psalm 127:1).

- Make an early commitment that you will not allow your children to absorb hours of violence on TV.

- Tell your children how special they are, how valuable and unique their lives are.

- Help your kids learn to value life.

7-12 Years

- Make it a family rule that no one goes to bed angry (Ephesians 4:26).

- Teach your children the link between anger and violence— you should have no problem finding examples!

• Warn your kids against resorting to their own revenge for wrongs done (Romans 12:19-21).

• Continue to keep a close check on your children's viewing and play habits, especially video games

13+ Years

• Help your teens understand what's involved in issues such as abortion and euthanasia.

• Help them find outlets for expressing their Christian views on these issues—perhaps taking part in a pro-life rally, writing letters, etc.

• Explain the difference between the Sixth Commandment and the issue of capital punishment.

• Encourage in your teens the development of a strong sense of right and wrong.

8

THE KEY TO A MAGNIFICENT MARRIAGE

Marital love plus absolute commitment and trust builds a sweet intimacy that is sublime.

—*R. Kent Hughes* [1]

I heard about an old couple sitting by the fireside. He looked over at her, had a romantic thought, and said, "After fifty years, I've found you tried and true."

The wife's hearing wasn't very good, so she said, "What?"

He repeated, "After fifty years, I've found you tried and true."

"After fifty years, I'm tired of you too," she replied.

I hope that's not how your marriage will be after fifty years. I want to show you how to have fifty years and more of a marriage that, by the grace of God, can be *magnificent*. God wants your marriage to be absolutely splendid, and the key is found in the Seventh Commandment. In Exodus 20:14 God's Word says with no stutter, no stammer, no apology, and no compromise, "Thou shalt not commit adultery."

Generations come and generations go, but the Ten Commandments stand. When it comes to God's standard for moral purity, it's time to remind ourselves that God's laws don't need to be amended or revised. We are broken on them if we try to break them. The Bible says, "His commandments are not grievous" (1 John 5:3). They are God's laws for liberty.

So when God says, "Thou shalt not commit adultery," we need to write that law on our hearts. If the law of God is only on the outside, it will be a rule, a regulation, a restraint. But if it's on the inside, if the righteousness of the law is fulfilled within us, then God's law brings us liberty and release.

The Great Wall of China was built over many hundreds of years to keep China's northern enemies from invading. The Great Wall is so wide that chariots could ride across the top. It is one of the few manmade objects that astronauts can see from outer space as they look back on the earth.

But the Great Wall did not keep the enemy out. Do you know why? All the enemy had to do was bribe a gatekeeper. Despite the massive wall, there was an enemy on the inside that let the enemy on the outside in. So it is in our lives. The gatekeeper of our hearts is on the inside. That gatekeeper must be faithful or the walls of restraint, the laws of God's Word, will do us no good.

AN ALL-ENCOMPASSING COMMANDMENT

The Seventh Commandment deals with all forms of immorality. What it says in a nutshell is that all sexual involvement outside of marriage, whether premarital or extramarital sex, is a grievous sin against Almighty God.

Back in the sixties we were told that the Ten Commandments, and especially this one, were out-of-date, old-fashioned. A so-called new morality, which was really the old immorality, was announced, and millions of young people followed it and were sucked into the swirling sewers of sin.

But the new morality exacted a huge toll on our society, and today we are paying the bill as sexually transmitted diseases ravage a generation and homes are coming apart at the seams. But the world continues to defy God's Commandments as immorality of all kinds comes out of the closet and into the glare of the public spotlight.

But God will not be mocked (Galatians 6:7). He has not canceled His statutes. The Seventh Commandment is repeated and reinforced throughout the New Testament. Jesus told the rich young ruler, "Thou shalt not commit adultery" (Matthew 19:18). First Corinthians 10:8 says, "Neither let us commit fornication." Paul wrote in Colossians 3:5,

"Mortify therefore your members which are upon the earth; fornication, uncleanness, inordinate affection, evil concupiscence." And in 1 Thessalonians 4:3 the apostle says, "This is the will of God, even your sanctification, that ye should abstain from fornication."

The word *fornication* means any sexual immorality, whether before or after marriage. If you are married and are sexually active with anyone other than your marriage partner, you are violating God's command. You are sinning against God and your partner, and you are inviting His judgment.

The Seventh Commandment also speaks to you if you are unmarried but sexually active. You are sinning against God and against the person you will marry. And you're building barriers that you will have to overcome after you get married.

So many of us who have children and grandchildren are wondering who our children will marry. Will there be a person who is sexually pure available for them to marry? How are our children going to find the right person? We must teach them to be the right person, because if they are the right person they will have a much greater hope of finding the right person.

In his famous book *Brave New World*, the English novelist Aldous Huxley satirized what he saw as the destruction of human values by the worship of science. In describing what he saw as the future of marriage, Huxley said the day would come when marriage licenses would be sold like dog licenses—good for a period of twelve months, with no law against changing dogs or keeping more than one animal at a time.

THE STATE OF MODERN MARRIAGE

Huxley wrote that in 1932, when I'm sure such a thought about marriage seemed preposterous. But now we're almost there. A marriage license is still a little harder to get than a dog license, but not much.

We have long since come to the point, though, that it's easier to get a marriage license than a driver's license. Think about it. All you have to do to get married is put your money down, apply for a license, pass a blood test, wait a few days, then have someone say a few words over you and pronounce you married.

But when our young people go to get a driver's license, they get a thick manual they have to study and pass a test on. Most of them go through a driver's education course that involves hours of classroom study and more hours in a car observing other student drivers and driving themselves under the watchful eye of an instructor. Then they have to pass a driving test with an officer in the car.

In other words, to get a driver's license young people have to know something. Imagine what would happen to today's marriages if engaged couples were given the "manual" on marriage, God's Word, when they applied for their license and then had to spend hours with "instructors," an older married couple who could help them get started right.

But marriage today is more often like a mountain with a beautiful valley at the bottom. I want you to picture the scene. There's a winding road coming down the mountainside, full of steep cliffs and sharp precipices. There are also obstacles in the road and few, if any, guardrails. At the top of the mountain, a car is starting down the road.

In that car are two newlyweds, heading toward the happy valley of blissful marriage. Along the way they pick up some passengers, but all along that road there are wrecks and other automobiles careening over the precipices or running into the obstacles.

The people in the other cars are being broken and maimed, and the passengers they've picked up along the way are being broken and crushed too. The couples driving those cars thought that when they started toward the happy valley, it was going to be a wonderful and easy trip. But something happened along the way.

That's an illustration of marriage in America today. What should we do? We need to have compassion on those whose cars have already crashed. We need to have a heart of love and kindness and let these broken people know that our hearts and churches are open to them. The Word of God has something to say to them. God loves them. They need to know that God is a God who forgives and restores through Jesus Christ and does not hold grudges.

We need to teach about God's love because there are a lot of broken people who don't need somebody pointing a finger in their face. They need somebody who will come alongside them and help bind up their wounds. I wouldn't want any reader to think that this book or this chapter in particular is meant to blame them or push them further down.

A second thing we need to do is to build some barricades, some guardrails along the road to the happy valley. We need to be removing some of the obstacles that are causing these disastrous marital wrecks. The laws of our land regarding divorce certainly need to be changed. It ought to be harder to get divorced than it is now. In fact, it ought to be harder to get married. Something should be required up-front in the way of counseling before two young people can get a marriage license.

Much in our society seems to work against stable and happy marriages. And the devil has leveled all of the artillery of hell against our homes. But we can prevent some of these wrecks if we will build guardrails.

But the main thing we need to do is teach young men and women how to "drive"! As I suggested above, engaged couples or newlyweds could benefit greatly from spending time with a happily married older couple. The church can help young people by faithfully teaching and modeling God's precepts for marriage.

We also need to teach and encourage our teenagers and unmarried young adults to stay sexually pure. I thank God for abstinence programs like True Love Waits and others that are challenging Christian young people to take a pledge of sexual purity before God.

So often what we have today in America is a vicious cycle of broken homes producing broken people who marry other broken people and produce new broken homes. But the cycle is not irreversible. We can break that cycle by showing our young people how to have godly marriages—how to get from the mountain to the happy valley without crashing.

We have a responsibility before God to help other people prepare for marriage. You can help your children choose happiness and obedience to God by teaching them His plan for a magnificent marriage.

GOD'S PLAN FOR MARRIAGE

What is God's plan for marriage? His Word gives it to us in just a few verses that contain in principle every problem a marriage will face and the answer to those problems:

> And the LORD God caused a deep sleep to fall upon Adam, and
> he slept; and he took one of his ribs, and closed up the flesh

instead thereof. And the rib, which the LORD God had taken from man, made he a woman, and brought her unto the man. And Adam said, This is now bone of my bones, and flesh of my flesh: she shall be called Woman, because she was taken out of Man. Therefore shall a man leave his father and his mother, and shall cleave unto his wife: and they shall be one flesh.

—Genesis 2:21-24

Here is all of marriage distilled down to its purest essence. Everything you need to know to teach your children how to make a magnificent marriage—and how to be successful in keeping the Seventh Commandment—is found in this text, especially in verse 24. Any marital advice we can give will simply be an enlargement or an extrapolation of that verse.

The Priority of Marriage

The verbs "leave" and "cleave" in Genesis 2:24 tell us that marriage has the highest priority. The highest priority in family life is not parent to child or child to parent, but mate to mate. The permanent union of marriage takes precedence over the temporary task of child-rearing.

Therefore, we as parents must be preparing our children to leave us, just as an eagle stirs her nest when it's time for her offspring to leave. We need to stir our nests so our children can go out and have a home of their own.

Now, those little eagles don't want to leave the nest. It's so comfortable in there, and the mother eagle comes with food and drops it in their mouths. But there comes a time when that young eagle must fly away from the nest.

But many parents don't want to have an empty nest, so they keep it feathered and make it easy for the children to stay where it's comfortable and everything is provided. That's a mistake. When we overly pamper our children, we're not equipping them to fly on their own. We're actually handicapping them when it comes to building successful homes themselves.

Parents who pamper their kids often excuse it by saying, "I just want to give my children all the things my parents were never able to give me."

That makes me wonder, are you giving your children the things your parents *did* give you? Here's what I mean.

I was raised in a home where we didn't have a lot of extra things. I grew up in the latter years of the Great Depression. We didn't have money to spend on luxuries. I never knew what it was to eat out. We were having enough trouble eating in!

But sometimes when my dad didn't have work to do, we'd go to Singer Island near our home in West Palm Beach, and we kids would catch minnows for Dad to fish with.

We would build a bonfire there on the beach, and Mom would bring two or three cans of pork and beans. We would fry the fish my father caught in Crisco and have a meal right there. Those are my best memories, things we did because we didn't have money to do anything else. Those were the times when, because we didn't have things, we worked together as a family.

The question is not whether you are giving your children the things your parents didn't give you. The question is, are you giving them the things your parents did give you? I'm talking about the values and commitments that make for magnificent marriages.

The Bible teaches that a priority must be placed on marriage. Your parents are not your supreme commitment. Your children are not your supreme commitment. After the Lord, your mate is your supreme commitment.

The Permanence of Marriage

Notice how Genesis 2:24 teaches the permanence of marriage as well. The Bible says the man "shall cleave unto his wife." The Hebrew word has the idea of joining or gluing two things together. It's not the partners in a marriage who glue themselves together. It's God who does this.

Jesus said in Mark 10:9, "What therefore God hath joined together, let not man put asunder." Marriage is permanent. Marriage is "'til death do us part." Show me two young people who consider divorce as an option, and I'll show you two young people who have a greatly increased potential for a breakup of their marriage.

People say, "We got divorced because we had problems." I have news for you. People who stay married and people who get divorced have basically the same kinds of problems. The difference is not in the problems. The difference is in the commitment to solving them.

Everybody has problems in marriage. You had better watch a man who says he understands women. He'll lie about other things too! One man walked into the kitchen and found his wife in tears. "I believe this is the worst meal I've ever cooked," she cried. "No, it isn't," he said, trying to console her.

It's dangerous being married! But get rid of the idea of divorce. Take your scissors and cut that word out of your mental dictionary. Divorce is the only game in which both players lose. No-fault divorce is a contradiction in terms.

All married people have problems. But why take the 90 percent of a marriage that is working fine and throw it away because of the 10 percent that's in trouble? That's simply a lack of commitment.

The Purpose of Marriage

Genesis 2:24 also speaks of the purpose of marriage: "they shall be one flesh." This deals with more than the sexual union of a husband and wife, though that is included. It means that they will be "one flesh" emotionally and spiritually as well.

Marriage is a romance in which both the hero and heroine die in the first chapter. But it's okay because they become one new person. Marriage is much like a violin. A violin without a bow produces no music. A bow without a violin also produces no music. But when the two come together, they make beautiful music. That's the way marriage is. God takes two people and makes them one.

Someone will say, "Oh, that's old-fashioned." Yes, but it's still mighty good. After more than thirty years of being told we need to be liberated from the Bible's outmoded ideas of love and marriage, guess what the latest polls show? They show that the best sexual relationships and the greatest emotional stability come to those who submit to God's standards and keep themselves pure for marriage.

A new study commissioned by the Family Research Council of Washington, D.C., found that the people most likely to report a high degree of satisfaction with their current sex life are married people who strongly believe that sex outside of marriage is wrong. The study found that 72 percent of these "married traditionalists" reported sexual satisfaction. This is 31 percent higher than unmarried non-traditionalists and 13 percent higher than married non-traditionalists. The study went on to show that sexually happy people also tend to go to church. Some two-thirds of the responders who attend church weekly are very satisfied with their sex lives, compared to barely half of those who never attend church.

Amazing! When all else fails, go back and read the directions. We are not smarter than God. Marriage is for more than the propagation of the race. It's for mutual love and comfort and joy.

God loves you, and when He says, "Thou shalt not commit adultery," He's not trying to keep you from sex. He is trying to keep sex for you. Sex is His wonderful gift to be enjoyed within marriage. "Marriage is honorable in all, and the bed undefiled: but whoremongers and adulterers God will judge" (Hebrews 13:4).

So if I may take you back to our mountain illustration, in order to get those newlyweds safely down the treacherous mountain road to the happy valley, we need to teach them God's plan for a magnificent marriage. His plan is very simple but all-inclusive. It involves the priority of marriage, the permanence of marriage, and the purpose of marriage. Then they will achieve the happiness, the satisfaction, the joy, and the fulfillment that God intended in spite of the difficulties along the way.

GOD'S WARNING ABOUT ADULTERY

There's a second thing you and I must do if we would help our children learn the secret to a successful home. We need to warn them about the harm and the heartbreak that come to those who violate God's Commandment. We would be less than fair to our children, and would not be handling the Word of God correctly, unless we warned them very solemnly and very sternly about the dangers of violating the Seventh Commandment. There's no equivocation when God says, "Thou shalt not commit adultery."

To adulterate means to make impure. When you adulterate the purity of singleness or the sanctity of marriage, you have made impure something that God values very highly. Let me show you why adultery is a grievous sin.

A Sin Against Yourself

Adultery is a sin against yourself. "Flee fornication. Every sin that a man doeth is without the body; but he that committeth fornication sinneth against his own body" (1 Corinthians 6:18). There's no sin that will do you more spiritual, psychological, and physical damage than immorality.

Lord Byron was handsome, witty, and charming. He was the playboy poet of England. But he died of venereal disease at an early age. This is what he wrote: "My days are in the yellow leaf. The flower and the fruits of life are gone. The worm, the canker, and the grief are mine alone." Byron had it all, but he lost it all through immorality.

Everyone is talking today about so-called safe sex. But sex is not supposed to be dangerous. It is supposed to be sacred. Adultery is a sin against your own body.

A Sin Against the Home

One of the most heinous things about adultery is what it does to a home and to the children in that home. The lives of innocent children are being torn apart in America by the sin of adultery.

Mothers and fathers who commit adultery are making a devastating statement to their children about how little they value their mate and how little fidelity means to them. They are also teaching their children that honor and commitment are not nearly as important as momentary pleasure. An adulterous parent is telling his or her children that pleasure is even more important to that parent than the children themselves. That's pretty stiff stuff, but it's true.

A Sin Against the Church

Adultery is also a sin against the church. "None of us liveth to himself, and no man dieth to himself," Paul said in Romans 14:7. The "us" he is talking about is the church, the people of God. The Bible also teaches that we are "the temple of God." Thus, "If any man defile the temple of God, him shall God destroy; for the temple of God is holy, which temple ye are" (1 Corinthians 3:16-17).

You say your sex life is your business? I beg to differ. If you're a member of the body of Christ, it's the business of the church too. My sex life is your business because we're in this together; we're members of the same body. When a believer lives in sexual immorality, he or she sins against the body of Christ. He takes the members of Christ and makes them members of a harlot. God forbid!

A Sin Against the Nation

Adultery is a sin against one's nation too. I wonder how long it will be before the wrath of our holy God falls on America. The great English historian Edward Gibbon, who wrote *The Decline and Fall of the Roman Empire*, said that immorality was the number one force that brought the mighty Roman Empire crashing down.

Historians tell us that immorality was also the sin that destroyed the ancient empires of Greece, Egypt, and Babylon. And it may well be the sin that destroys America. Even now the torrents of God's wrath are pounding hard against the dam of His mercy. One day that dam will give way to the waters of God's judgment.

The Bible says, "Righteousness exalteth a nation: but sin is a reproach to any people" (Proverbs 14:34). The Law of Moses said to the nation of Israel living under the theocracy:

> If a man be found lying with a woman married to a husband, then they shall both of them die, both the man that lay with the woman, and the woman: so shalt thou put away evil from Israel.
> —Deuteronomy 22:22

God said to put away this evil from the nation so that the nation could survive. The enemy of the home is the enemy of society, and people who treat sex lightly will treat other people lightly. Immorality can bring down an entire society.

A Sin Against God

But here's the bottom line: it is Almighty God who said, "Thou shalt not commit adultery." When David committed adultery, he was wise enough to pray in Psalm 51:4, "Against thee, thee only, have I sinned, and done this evil in thy sight."

Proverbs 6:32 says, "Whoso committeth adultery with a woman lacketh understanding: he that doeth it destroyeth his own soul." Why does the adulterer destroy his own soul? Because he has sinned against

God. The Ten Commandments are not advice. They are holy laws, and the penalty and consequences for disobedience are serious indeed.

Don't get the idea that a pure life is just an option you may choose as a Christian. If you're not living a life of sexual purity, you have no right to call yourself a Christian. I didn't say that. Look at what the Bible says:

> Know ye not that the unrighteous shall not inherit the kingdom of God? Be not deceived: neither fornicators, nor idolaters, nor adulterers, nor effeminate, nor abusers of themselves with mankind . . . shall inherit the kingdom of God.
>
> —1 Corinthians 6:9-10

> This ye know, that no whoremonger, nor unclean person . . . hath any inheritance in the kingdom of Christ and of God.
>
> —Ephesians 5:5

> But the fearful, and unbelieving, and the abominable, and murderers, and whoremongers . . . shall have their part in the lake which burneth with fire and brimstone: which is the second death.
>
> —Revelation 21:8

No matter how you glamorize it, God says immorality is a sin against Him. Someone may say, "I'm a member of the church, and I'm living that way, and nothing has happened to me." Such a person may not be a legitimate member of God's family (see Hebrews 12:8). God says, "If you are My child, I will chastise you." According to Romans 2:5, anyone who sins with a hard and unrepentant heart is "treasur[ing] up" God's "wrath" upon himself.

MODELING GOD'S COMMANDMENT

We need to teach our children God's standard for purity. We need to warn them against breaking the Seventh Commandment. We need to model sexual purity before our children.

Such *modeling* first involves making a personal decision for Christ. We must make sure that we have given our hearts to Christ. No matter what your sin or failure, He will forgive, and He will not hold grudges.

Every stain, every blot, every blemish He will bury in the sea of God's for-getfulness when you come to Jesus for cleansing.

A second aspect of modeling is *dependence*. Let your children see that you have not only made a decision to trust Christ, but that you depend on Him daily for the strength to remain pure in your marriage and in all of your relationships.

Make sure your children understand that Christ doesn't merely for-give us and then say, "Now try to do better." He comes to live within us, and His Holy Spirit offers to energize us and fill us with power for day-to-day obedience to God's commands.

The third component of modeling sexual purity is *devotion*. Pour out your love to Christ and to your family. God gives us a supernatural love for others. Godly love is not simply an emotion you turn on and off.

When a man comes to me and says, "I'm going to divorce my wife because I don't love her anymore," he gets no sympathy from me. Why? Because love is a decision, not an emotional impulse over which we have no control.

God has commanded us to love. Anybody can love who chooses to love. When the Bible says, "Husbands, love your wives" (Ephesians 5:25), that's not a suggestion. So no Christian can legitimately say he or she has fallen out of love with his or her marriage partner and can't go on. We can decide to love.

Development is the fourth step in modeling purity before our chil-dren. Let your love continue to grow. Even though we use a diamond to represent love, true love is really not like a diamond. That is, love is not some precious gem that we acquire and treasure. That's a static thing. Love is more like a flower. It must be cultivated and nurtured so it can grow.

If a man doesn't love his wife more now than the day they got mar-ried, he loves her less. Love is never static. I ask young couples when I marry them, "Will you continue to feed your love from day to day, week to week, and year to year with the very best you have to give?"

Men, never start flirting with another woman. And never stop flirt-ing with your wife. Do those little things that mean so much. Keep the "honey" in the honeymoon.

The next aspect of being a godly model is *discipline*. Guard your company. Friends who urge you to sin are not friends. Watch what you put in front of your eyes. If you sit in front of the television "channel surfing" with your remote control, things are going to appear on the screen that you should not be watching.

You wouldn't put garbage in your mouth. Why put it in your brain? And don't say it won't affect you. "Can a man take fire in his bosom, and his clothes not be burned?" (Proverbs 6:27). Watch what you watch.

When I was in college, I had this motto on my desk: "He who would not fall down ought not to walk in slippery places." I needed that word of warning then, and I need it now. So do you. The Bible says, "Flee fornication" (1 Corinthians 6:18). There must be discipline in your life.

Finally, you need *determination* to be the kind of example you need to be. Make up your mind that you are going to be true to God and to your mate. I don't have to make up my mind every time I go out of town whether or not I'm going to be true to Joyce. I don't have to make up my mind every time I turn on the television whether I'm going to watch filth or not, or whether I'm going to buy something filthy every time I pass a newsstand. Why? I have already made up my mind about that.

I'm not saying that to be arrogant. I'm simply saying that my heart is fixed on the Lord. I have decided to follow Jesus. Perhaps you have too. You will still face temptation, but that deep determination in your heart is an anchor to your soul. Say with Joshua, "As for me and my house, we will serve the LORD" (Joshua 24:15).

God's plan, God's command, is purity, both inside and outside of marriage. If you've failed, God will forgive you if you come to Him with an open and repentant heart. If you have a broken heart or a broken home, bring it to Jesus. He can put it back together if you give Him all the pieces.

Remember the woman taken in adultery? Jesus exposed the hypocrisy of her accusers, then forgave her and said, "Go, and sin no more" (John 8:11). We need to be like the Savior and forgive those who have fallen.

The first miracle our Lord ever performed was at a wedding (John 2:1-11). The good news is, He is still performing miracles at weddings! When you commit yourself to obey God, He can give you a magnificent marriage. Decide and determine to keep yourself pure before Him, and watch how He will bless you.

TURNING THE COMMANDMENTS INTO COMMITMENTS

0-6 Years

- Begin praying now for godly mates for your children.
- Start teaching your children the sanctity and value of their bodies as created by and belonging to God.
- Be careful to be modest in dress and behavior before your children, without being afraid to show affection to your mate.

7-12 Years

- Recount the story of how you and your marriage partner met and fell in love. Make it a family legend.
- Make it a point to talk about the value of waiting— the joy of marital fulfillment.
- Help your children notice and appreciate good traits in others— not just physical beauty.

13+ Years

- Pray that your teens will be emotionally and spiritually prepared to handle relationships with the opposite sex.
- Never treat sex as a dirty or embarrassing subject.
- Promise that you will answer honestly any questions your children have about sex.
- Challenge your teens to take a vow of purity until marriage. Give them a ring or some other token of their vow.

9

HONESTY: DON'T LEAVE HOME WITHOUT IT

A person doesn't have to be dishonest simply because it is the accepted way. Being right is worth far more than being accepted.

—Donald Wildmon [1]

America has forgotten the basic rules of honesty. I read about a market in California where a little boy was standing in front of the fruit stand, cramming grapes into his mouth as fast as he could. His mother was nowhere in sight.

A clerk was standing by helplessly, not knowing what to do as this little fellow pigged out on the grapes. After a while his mother appeared and saw what was happening. Unfortunately, the only thing she said to him by way of reproof was, "Johnny, don't eat so fast."

This is the kind of society we live in. We seem to have forgotten the basic rules of honesty expressed so clearly in the Eighth Commandment: "Thou shalt not steal" (Exodus 20:15). You don't need to have a doctorate to understand that command. If there was ever a truth needed today, this is it. It's one of God's ancient secrets to a successful home, a principle that is written loud and clear in the pages of Scripture.

God's Word tells us that any time we take anything that belongs to someone else or withhold that which rightly belongs to another, we have transgressed this Commandment. We're going to see that whether it's time, money, affection, possessions, appreciation, love, or anything else, if we defraud somebody else in the matter, we are guilty of stealing.

When God gave His law to the children of Israel, He told parents to teach these things to their children and grandchildren. How can we teach our children what the Eighth Commandment means? By teaching them what it means to live with honesty and integrity.

To do that, I want to lay another verse alongside Exodus 20:15. It is Ephesians 4:28, which in my estimation is the perfect explanation and amplification of this Commandment:

> Let him that stole steal no more: but rather let him labor, work-
> ing with his hands the thing which is good, that he may have to
> give to him that needeth.

This is a dynamite verse, packed with three grand principles that need to be emblazoned on the heart of every child and etched into our children's consciousness, so they will discover God's secret for successful homes.

The first principle is integrity: "Let him that stole steal no more." The second is industry: "Let him labor, working with his hands the thing which is good." And the third is generosity: "That he may have to give to him that needeth."

All of these principles are wrapped up in the Commandment that says, "Thou shalt not steal." Here are three characteristics that should make all of us pray, "Dear God, help me to teach these things to my children, and help me to practice them before my children."

THE NECESSITY OF INTEGRITY

There are many ways you can live without integrity. Let's talk about the problem and consider some solutions.

Direct Theft

The most obvious violation of the Eighth Commandment is direct steal-ing through crimes such as shoplifting, armed robbery, and burglary.

Our cities are plagued with these things. Shoplifting touches the home more directly because many children and young people are committing this crime as a sort of prank or on a dare.

But retail stores and private homes are not the only crime scenes. Stealing at the workplace is epidemic. The American economy loses $40 billion annually from theft on the job. That's everything from pilfering to embezzlement in the workplace. Direct stealing, whether in a store or on the job, will receive the sure judgment of Almighty God.

Fraud

Another form of stealing is fraud, or what we call white-collar crime. Many of us raised our children on a brand of baby food from one of the major baby food manufacturers in the country. For many years parents trusted this company and its products as an emblem of purity and good nourishment for their babies and young children.

Then one day it was discovered that the apple juice this company had been selling for ten years, and which they had advertised as 100 percent fruit juice, was little more than chemicals and dye and water—sort of a chemical cocktail.

The company was told not to sell this product anymore—don't let mothers think they're giving their babies apple juice when they are really giving them a chemical concoction. What did the company do with the juice? They loaded nine tractor trailers with the stuff, and within days it was being sold in Puerto Rico, the Dominican Republic, and the Virgin Islands.[2]

I read about a motel in Alabama that offers a $20 cash rebate on its rooms, which are $80. A salesman could stay at that motel, receive an immediate $20 to put in his pocket, and get a receipt for the $80 room bill. Then he could submit that receipt on his expense account and be reimbursed for the $80.[3] That's fraud, and it's a form of stealing.

Halfhearted work is also stealing. If you don't give your employer an honest day's labor, you've stolen from him. Colossians 3:22 says, "Servants, obey in all things your masters according to the flesh; not with eyeservice, as menpleasers; but in singleness of heart, fearing God." If you don't fear God enough to give your employer an honest day's work, you have broken God's Commandment.

I heard about a man who was applying for a job. He asked his prospective employer, "How much will you pay me?" The employer replied, "I'll pay you what you're worth." "Oh, no, nothing doing," the man said. "I just quit a job making more than that." I'm afraid there are a lot of people being paid more than they're worth.

Now, the truth of this Commandment cuts both ways. If you're an employer and you don't pay your employees what they're worth, you have stolen from them. Look ahead just a few more verses in Colossians and you will read, "Masters [employers], give unto your servants that which is just and equal; knowing that ye also have a Master in heaven" (4:1).

Business owner, do you pay the people who work for you, including the domestic worker in your home, what is "just and equal"? One way to judge this is to ask yourself, if you were in their place, would you expect to be paid more than you pay them? James 5:4 is a sobering verse: "Behold, the hire of the laborers who have reaped down your fields, which is of you kept back by fraud, crieth: and the cries of them which have reaped are entered into the ears of the Lord of Sabaoth."

God knows when an employer doesn't pay his workers what he ought to pay. Notice the title James uses for God. "The Lord of Sabaoth" is the Lord God Almighty, the Sovereign Ruler whose job it is to right wrongs.

Some people who are breaking the Eighth Commandment simply think of themselves as shrewd in business. Tax planning is one thing, but tax evasion is something else. Having insurance is one thing, but insurance fraud is something else. Jesus warned about the scribes who "devour widows' houses" (Mark 12:38-40). They sought opportunities to take advantage of defenseless and unsuspecting widows who did not know how to protect themselves.

Gambling

Isn't it sad that one of the greatest forms of thievery in America is perfectly legal in so many places? Let's set the record straight on the gambling industry—it's thievery, every bit of it.

Gambling is morally wrong. Why? Because nobody can win at gambling without somebody else losing. Legitimate business is win/win.

For instance, suppose I make a widget and sell it to you for one dollar. I get the dollar. You get the widget. We both win. But in gambling, for every winner there must be countless losers. You can't bet a dollar and win a million dollars unless an awful lot of people bet dollars that in many cases they can't afford to lose.

Gambling builds up false hope, a perversion of true hope. It promises happiness but delivers disappointment and frustration. Therefore, gambling is profit and pleasure at the cost of somebody else's pain and loss. It's an attempt to get what belongs to someone else without giving him anything for it. That fits any definition of stealing we can write.

If two people meet in an alley and one points a gun at the other and takes his money, they call it robbery. But if two people meet in a casino and one takes the other person's money, they call it "gaming." That sounds so much better than "gambling."

Someone might object, "Wait a minute. There's a big difference between a robbery and someone playing in a casino. The person in the alley is being robbed against his will. But no one's forcing anyone to gamble. The person in the casino is a willing participant."

But the fact that gambling is done willingly doesn't make it right. A dual, for instance, is merely murder by mutual consent. Just because two people agree to shoot each other according to some silly set of rules doesn't give either one the right to take another's life.

The person who gambles and wins has the spirit of thievery. The person who gambles and loses is operating with the same wrong motive, but he has the added problem of being very foolish. We must warn our children about the evils of gambling, because they are going to face it everywhere they turn. The Bible says, "Woe to him that increaseth that which is not his!" (Habakkuk 2:6).

Withholding Love

Withholding our love and devotion from those to whom it is due also causes us to break this Commandment. For example, the Bible commands husbands and wives not to defraud each other in the matter of sexual love (1 Corinthians 7:5).

We are also commanded not to withhold neighborly love. "Owe no man any thing, but to love one another" (Romans 13:8). "Thou shalt love thy neighbor as thyself," Jesus said (Matthew 22:39). We owe others love.

Some children have defrauded their parents of honor. Some parents have defrauded their children of proper guidance, love, and instruction. But God's Word says, "Thou shalt not steal."

Stealing from Yourself

When we steal from others by any of the means we have just discussed—whether it be flagrant robbery, a crooked business deal, or failing to love as we ought—do you know who we are really stealing from? Ourselves.

When you fail in these other ways, you are also robbing yourself. The Bible says, "Your iniquities have turned away these things, and your sins have withholden good things from you" (Jeremiah 5:25). You defraud yourself when you attempt to defraud others. In seeking to get, you're the one who loses. It pays to serve Jesus every day, every step of the way.

Stealing from God

But the worst form of thievery is to steal from God. You say, "How can we steal from God?"

Have you given Him your life? Then You belong to Him. "Ye are not your own. . . . Ye are bought with a price" (1 Corinthians 6:19-20).

You are God's by creation. He made you. You are also His by redemption. He gave Christ to die for you—the greatest price of all. When you live for self and self alone, you are stealing from God. When you walk God's green earth, breathe His air, and live with the life He gave you without pouring that life back out in devotion to Him, the Bible says you are a thief.

We tithe because the tithe is a symbol that everything we have belongs to God. But don't get the idea that only 10 percent of what you have belongs to God. *Everything* you have belongs to Him. The One who owns the sheep owns the wool. Since you belong to God, all that you have really belongs to Him. He is simply loaning it to you for a time.

To withhold from God that which is rightfully His is robbery of the worst sort. God Himself asked the people of Israel in Malachi 3:8, "Will a man rob God? Yet ye have robbed me. But ye say, Wherein have we robbed thee? In tithes and in offerings." Don't be found guilty of keeping back for yourself what is God's.

THE IMPORTANCE OF INDUSTRY

Along with integrity, we also need to teach our children industry. Remember what Ephesians 4:28 says. Rather than stealing, "let him labor, working with his hands the thing which is good."

The Blessing of Work

Work is not bad. It is good, a gift from God. Work is not a curse. Work is a blessing. The Bible is very clear about the importance of work. Paul laid down this rule: "If any would not work, neither should he eat" (2 Thessalonians 3:10).

The ancient Jews understood that the Fourth Commandment mandating a day of rest was based upon the premise, "Six days shalt thou labor, and do all thy work" (Exodus 20:9). They knew that work was as important as rest. The old rabbis used to say, "He who does not teach his son a trade teaches him to steal."

The rabbis saw work as a gift from God. So did the writer of Ecclesiastes:

> Behold that which I have seen: it is good and comely for one to eat and to drink, and to enjoy the good of all his labor that he taketh under the sun all the days of his life, which God giveth him: for it is his portion. Every man also to whom God hath given riches and wealth, and hath given him power to eat thereof, and to take his portion, and to rejoice in his labor; this is the gift of God.
>
> —5:18-19

Work and the rewards that it brings are God's good gifts to us, meant to be savored and enjoyed.

A Lost Generation

The problem with this generation is that by and large our young people do not know either the importance or the value of honest labor. We have young men and women graduating from college today who still don't know how to make a living. People want to win the lottery or the sweepstakes so they won't have to work anymore. But that would be a pathetic way to live.

Let me say a word here that may sound political. I hope not, because I believe it's moral and biblical. You cannot legislate the poor into freedom by legislating the industrious out of it. You don't multiply wealth by dividing it. Government cannot give anything to anybody that it doesn't first take from somebody else.

Whenever somebody receives something without working for it, somebody else has to work for it without receiving. The worst thing that can happen to a nation is for half of the people to get the idea they don't have to work because somebody else will work for them, and the other half to get the idea that it does no good to work because they don't get to enjoy the fruit of their labor.

Something very sad has happened in America. The hippies and flower children of the sixties—who went around smoking dope, crying out about peace and free love, and urging kids to "turn on, tune in, and drop out"—took off their tattered jeans and their beads, trimmed their hair, put on suits, and went to Washington.

But they took with them their hippie philosophy that the only dirty four-letter word is *work*. So what we have is the biggest cultural revolution in America's history. We raised a generation that did not understand or value the work ethic. And they turned their philosophy into legislation.

The result is that America is still suffering today from the lack of a biblical work ethic. And even many of those who are working are not working for the pleasure and the joy of cooperating with Almighty God. They're only working to get enough money so they can stop working.

The Socialists had the badly flawed idea that all you had to do was pool a nation's wealth and turn everyone into a worker for the state. If you want to see the dismal failure of that philosophy, just walk the gray streets of Moscow as I have done and see Russia's crumbling infrastructure.

When I was in Russia our guide told us, "You know what was wrong with communism? Under communism we pretended to work, and they pretended to pay us, and everything went under."

Do you know what's wrong in America today? We have created a society perilously close to that description, a society in which some people are better off by not working.

Consider this scenario: a young girl is living in a poverty-stricken home infested with roaches and filth. She's afraid of the men in the house, and she's fighting with her mother all the time.

This girl wants to get out of that house, and her government has told her, "When you are sixteen, we will help you get your own apartment. Not only that—we will give you free legal aid, a welfare check, and food stamps."

But to receive all this there are two requirements. First, she must have a baby out of wedlock; she can't have a husband around to support her. And second, she must not get a job. Now if she meets those two requirements, our government will help her.[4] I am not trying to be hard on people. I am trying to be truthful. That's the worst thing we could do to our society.

God knows we have need to have mercy on those who are locked into this kind of a situation. But it is time for us to wake up and find another plan, because the old plan of no work has not worked, is not working now, and will never work.

Teaching the Value of Work

We need to teach our boys and girls how to work. A recent move in Alabama to put prison inmates to work caused a real furor. Imagine, making inmates work and maybe learning a skill! Did you know that in 1828 approximately 85 percent of all prison inmates were gainfully employed? But by 1990 less than 10 percent of those in prison worked.[5] Charles Colson says:

> With one of the most destructive and wasteful national policies imaginable, we are deliberately keeping almost a million men and women out of the labor force and denying them the skills they will need when they are released from prison to reenter the labor force.

Colson went on to say:

> I see these men locked in a narrow cell, lying on their bunks, staring at the ceiling, nothing to do. They live in a six-by-nine cage with a tiny black-and-white television set, a few books, and

absolutely nothing to do. We've seen the sullen expressions, the downcast eyes, the simmering bitterness.[6]

Isn't it sad to think of a person not learning how to work until they go to prison (if they learn it even there)? Many of the young people who are in prison never learned how to work. What went wrong?

Many of today's prison inmates didn't have a father who taught them a trade and modeled the value of honest, rewarding labor. They didn't have a mother who taught them the value of work by requiring them to help out with the household chores. They never knew what it means to be industrious.

Let's move to the other end of life's spectrum. Too many people are looking forward to retirement so they can finally sit back and do nothing. May God have mercy upon the pitiful soul who believes that line. You should never retire from serving God. If you are well enough off so that you don't have to go work tomorrow, that just gives you more time to serve God with all your heart and all your soul.

The opposite of productive work is idleness, and the Bible has nothing good to say about idleness. God never meant for any of us to idle away our days. Inactivity in retirement usually leads to boredom and a sense of uselessness. And that is a ticket to an early grave for many retirees.

Teaching Our Kids to Work

If you want to have a home that is successful in God's eyes, and if you want to help your children have the same, start early in teaching them industry. Lamentations 3:27 is a good verse to memorize and teach to your children: "It is good for a man that he bear the yoke in his youth." That means you don't have to wait until your children are grown to teach them what it means to work. In fact, you'd better not wait until they are grown to start this or it will never happen.

We often hear things like, "After all, play is a child's work. So just let the children play." Well, I'm not exactly advocating child labor! But even the smallest child can do a little something to help out and gain that sense of satisfaction and accomplishment that only comes from a job well done.

I've known what it is to work since I was a child. When I was in grammar school and junior high school, I bought my own clothes with the money I earned. I ran a milk route and did a day's work before the other kids were getting out of bed. In fact, I used to deliver milk to the girl I'm married to. Joyce would go look out the window to watch me set the milk down on her back porch.

I'm not bragging about this. The point is, the hard work didn't hurt me. My dad believed that his boys ought to work. My brother and I had to cut the grass. We had a kind of grass called "bitter blue" in our front yard in Florida. And when Dad would tell me to cut the grass, I was both bitter and blue!

We had an old push mower, not a power mower. And our edger didn't have string and a motor. It was one of those half-moon shovels that worked on foot power only. My brother and I would work on that lawn all day, and then my dad would come home and inspect it. When he'd say, "Boys, that's a good job. That really looks good," I would feel great. I felt like I had accomplished something and had helped earn my way.

I worked my way through college by cleaning tables. I've also been a carpenter's helper, an elevator mechanic, a used-car salesman, and a fruit picker. And I give God the praise that during four years of college and four years of seminary, I provided enough for my family that Joyce was able to stay home. And I graduated from seminary without owing anybody anything.

I give God the glory for that. I knew how to work as a teenager and then as a young husband because I learned how to work as a child. I'm so glad my father taught me how to work.

Helping Our Children Work

As a parent, I know that sometimes it's easier to do the job yourself than to get your child going and help him or her do it. But getting the job done is not the only goal here. There's no question that you can collect the trash twice in the time it takes you to help your child do it once. But helping him learn to work is the goal, not demonstrating your speed.

Give your children work to do, and if necessary help them get it done. And remember that school and afterschool activities are part of a child's work—homework, paper routes, baby-sitting, music lessons, sports practices, or whatever else. These are great opportunities for teaching children to stay with a job until it is finished.

Let me say again, I am not against children playing. But many kids and young people spend their summers complaining about how bored they are, that there's nothing to do. Around my house I was afraid to act bored, because my dad would find something for me to do. Help your children work at their appropriate level, and their play will be a whole lot sweeter.

THE JOY OF GENEROSITY

Here's my third and final point in this matter of obeying the Eighth Commandment and teaching your children to do the same. Just as Ephesians 4:28 teaches integrity and industry, it also teaches generosity: "Let him labor . . . that he may have to give to him that needeth."

Meeting Needs

The opposite of stealing is not simply not stealing. The opposite of taking from others what you have not earned is giving to others what you have earned. We need to teach our children to work, not only to meet their own needs, but to help meet the needs of others. Look at what Paul says in Acts 20:33-35:

> I have coveted no man's silver, or gold, or apparel. Yea, ye your-
> selves know, that these hands have ministered unto my necessi-
> ties, and to them that were with me. I have showed you all things,
> how that so laboring ye ought to support the weak, and to
> remember the words of the Lord Jesus, how he said, It is more
> blessed to give than to receive.

It's a sin and a shame before God that we expect the government to take care of our parents and our children when we ourselves ought to do it. Working with integrity and industry so we can give to others frees us from a life of selfishness. Children who learn to be selfish are going to be miserable adults. Misery comes from mirrors; but joy comes from windows, when we open our lives and begin to give to others.

Try a little experiment if you will. Squeeze your fist as tightly as you can and hold it while you read the next few sentences.

This is the way many people live. They go through life grasping what's theirs until it hurts. But God says we are to open our hands and give to those in need.

Now relax your hand. Doesn't that feel a lot better? That's the relief that comes to a generous giver.

Givers and Takers

There are only two kinds of people on this planet: givers and takers. Teach your children to give, and they will give you so much. Give them understanding, and they'll give you understanding. Teach them how to care, and they'll return that care.

People today want somebody to understand and to care. They will call a 900 number and pay a strange voice to pretend that he or she is listening and is interested in them.

John Wesley, the founder of Methodism, said something very profound: "Make all you can, save all you can, and give all you can." That's the integrity, the industry, and the generosity of honest work.

Teach your children to give out of their own money to God's work. If you give them an allowance, make sure they give from that allowance, even if it's only a nickel or a dime. Help your children discover the joy of bringing their money to church to give to the work of God.

Let your children participate in mission projects. Teach them how to give to their brothers and sisters. Train them in giving by precept and by your example.

Giving Yourself

Jesus poured out His life's blood for you on the cross. He suffered and died for you. He bought you. You belong to Him. Don't steal from God by withholding yourself from full surrender and full service to the Lord Jesus Christ. If I had a thousand lives to live, I'd give every one of them to Jesus.

All of the toys of this world that we cling to so possessively are going to be left behind someday. When I was a kid, I used to hear the saying, "Finders keepers, losers weepers." But Jesus says, "Keepers weepers, losers finders." His exact words were, "Whosoever shall lose his life for my sake and the gospel's, the same shall save it" (Mark 8:35).

Do you know what you ought to do if you've never done it? You ought to open your heart to Christ and say, "Lord Jesus, I give myself to You. I don't want to steal from You. The very life I have belongs to You, and I give it to You here and now."

When you give yourself to Jesus, He gives something back to you— abundant and eternal life (John 10:10). The Bible says we can't even begin to comprehend what He has in store for us (1 Corinthians 2:9). Whatever you may give up for Him cannot compare to the joy of what He gives to you!

TURNING THE COMMANDMENTS INTO COMMITMENTS

0-6 Years

- Model a spirit of contentment before your children. They will pick up your attitude very quickly.

- Begin now dealing with your little ones' "I want this" syndrome. Explain that we can't have everything we want, and be prepared to reinforce this lesson often!.

- Teach your child to be grateful. Stop and thank God for a good meal, sunshine, or any number of daily blessings.

7-12 Years

- Take the opportunity to point out things like store signs that warn against shoplifting, and use them as a discussion starter on the importance of honesty.

- Give your children "What would you do?" role-playing situations that call for a decision on honesty.

- Don't get caught in the game of buying your kids things to keep them quiet or to relieve your guilt for not spending more time with them or failing to keep a promise.

13+ Years

- Let your older children make their own decisions as appropriate.

- Don't bail them out if they overspend and run short for something they want to buy or do.

- Show them them how the real world works by showing them the difference between "gross" and "net" pay.

- Measure your own "honesty quotient" regularly.

10

TRUTH OR CONSEQUENCES

Lying has become a cultural trait in America. Lying is embedded in our national character.

—R. Kent Hughes [1]

I said at the beginning of Chapter Nine that America has lost its sense of basic honesty. It seems that we as a people have set aside and disregarded the Ninth Commandment, which says, "Thou shalt not bear false witness against thy neighbor" (Exodus 20:16).

Well, I'm happy to say that there are outstanding exceptions. Let me tell you an amazing story about one such person, a godly man who used to be on the pastoral staff at our church in Memphis.

This man and his grown sons were big fans of the Atlanta Braves baseball team. He had promised his sons back when they were young that if the Braves ever made it into the World Series, he would take them to a Series game, no matter what it cost.

Well, the Braves reached the World Series for the first time in the early 1990s. So this man called his sons and said, "We're going." He didn't have tickets, but he was determined to take his sons because he had promised them this ever since they were boys.

So my dear friend and his sons flew to Atlanta for the World Series. He knew they could get tickets from somebody, even if they had to buy tickets on the street for more than their face value from ticket scalpers.

When they got to Atlanta, this man read in the newspaper that it was against the law to scalp tickets, a fact he had not realized previously. Now he was faced with a moral dilemma. He and his sons had already flown to Atlanta. They already had their hotel room. What should they do now?

They talked about it and reasoned that it didn't say it was against the law to *buy* scalped tickets—just to *sell* them. So if they bought tickets from a scalper, they wouldn't be breaking the law—the scalper would.

But the Holy Spirit spoke to this dear father and said, "You know you are just playing with words. If it's against the law to sell the tickets at inflated prices, it's against the law to buy them."

So he told his sons they couldn't break the law and violate their integrity just to see a ball game. Since they were already there and they had no other way to get in, they decided to just stand in the parking lot at the ballpark and see if somebody had tickets they would sell at the regular price.

It was a crazy plan, but as they were standing there, a man came up to them and asked, "What are you folks doing here?" They explained their problem—and he had a solution!

This man was an official in the Atlanta Braves organization. He invited my friend and his sons to be his guests at the game. They were ushered into the area where the Braves' executives sit. He loaded them down with souvenirs and introduced them all around. Then they enjoyed the game from the executive suite.

What had happened was so incredible, they were still trying to get over it when they went back to their hotel. There the hotel manager came up to them and told them that because the staff was late cleaning their room, they would not receive a bill.

Don't get the wrong idea. You don't get a free ride every time you hold to your integrity. But it's exciting to see God at work when we refuse to compromise the truth. I want to help you teach your children to love honesty, to speak and live the truth. But we need to do a little blasting before we can build. So let's talk about the loss of absolute truth, then see from God's Word what we can do about it.

THE LOSS OF ABSOLUTE TRUTH

If America is indeed at the sad stage where honesty is being trampled in the dust, how did we get here? The social critics say it is an alarming decline in basic honesty. I say it's much more fundamental than that. We have lost the concept of absolute, God-given truth.

The problem is not a lack of information. We know more and believe less today than ever. We're drowning in a sea of facts. In the last thirty years, we've produced more information than in the previous 5,000 years. Nearly 50,000 books and 10,000 magazines are published in America every year. We're told that a person who reads a newspaper such as the *Los Angeles Times* gets more information in that one newspaper than a person who lived in the sixteenth century would get in a year. And information is said to be doubling every five years.

Those are the facts, but facts are no substitute for the truth. The so-called information superhighway is becoming a highway to hell because truth has been jettisoned along the way.

That's the world's word on truth. But what does God's Word have to say about all this? Look at Isaiah 59:14—"Judgment is turned away backward, and justice standeth afar off: for truth is fallen in the street, and equity cannot enter." This is a picture of a traffic jam. Here are judgment, justice, and equity all backed up, and they can't get through.

Why? Because truth has fallen. How did truth fall? She has been knocked down by professors of philosophy. She has been tripped by dishonest politicians. She has been chloroformed by liberal preachers. So truth lies "fallen in the street." This is a picture of America at the end of the twentieth century. Our job is to set truth back on her feet. If we don't tell the truth, we will assuredly pay the consequences.

THE LIABILITY OF A FALSE WITNESS

Who is the father, the source, of all false witness? It's Satan himself. Jesus said to the unsaved Pharisees:

> Ye are of your father the devil, and the lusts of your father ye will do: he was a murderer from the beginning, and abode not in the truth, because there is no truth in him. When he speaketh a lie, he speaketh of his own: for he is a liar, and the father of it.
>
> —John 8:44

Every time you tell a lie, you're acting like the devil. You need to understand this in no uncertain terms, and you need to communicate this vital truth to your children. Lies aren't funny or clever; they aren't "black" or "white." They are sin, every one of them. What are some of the sins of the tongue for which God holds us liable?

Slander

Why does lying about someone else make you like the devil? Because the very word *devil* means "slanderer." So when you bear false witness, when you slander, you're like the devil. But when you tell the truth, you're like the Lord Jesus, who is "the truth" (John 14:6).

Notice what Satan has done with his slander. In the Garden of Eden he used slander to corrupt our first parents. Satan slandered God's character and God's honesty, because God had told Adam concerning the tree of the knowledge of good and evil, "In the day that thou eatest thereof thou shalt surely die" (Genesis 2:17).

Eve repeated God's command to the devil when he tempted her, but he said, "Ye shall not surely die" (Genesis 3:4). The devil made God out to be a liar. He accused God of base motives, saying, "God doth know that in the day ye eat thereof, then your eyes shall be opened, and ye shall be as gods, knowing good and evil" (verse 5). In other words, "God doesn't really care about you. He's holding out on you."

The devil slandered the honesty and the goodness of God. Anyone who puts a question mark on the Word of God is doing the work of the devil. In the Garden of Eden the slanderer did his work, and Adam and Eve sinned. He corrupted them through his lies.

Satan also used slander and false witness to criticize the godly man Job. In Job 1 we see Satan appearing before the throne of God. Job's name is raised, and Satan begins to slander him.

Job was an upright man who loved God with all of his heart. So God said to Satan, "Hast thou considered my servant Job?" (Job 1:8). But Satan came right back with a terrible assault on Job's character.

Satan said in effect, "He doesn't really love You, God. The only reason he serves You is because You have bribed him. You've bought him off. You've given him all these good things. He's never known any heartache. He's never known any trouble. He's playing You for a sucker. He just serves You for what he can get out of You" (see Job 1:10).

To attack God's people is one thing, but Satan was not content with that. He even came against the Lord Jesus Christ Himself, the God-man, with his lies and temptations in the wilderness (see Matthew 4:1-11).

But it's at the end of Jesus' earthly life that we see the devil most clearly in his role as slanderer. When Jesus was arrested and brought to trial before the religious leaders of Israel, "The chief priests, and elders, and all the council, sought false witness against Jesus, to put him to death" (Matthew 26:59).

After digging through the human refuse of Jerusalem, they finally found two men who were willing accomplices of the devil, and those men delivered their false testimony (verses 60-61). The leaders seized on this to condemn Jesus to death.

So Satan has been bearing false witness against Jesus for a long time, and he's still doing it today. Anytime you hear someone deny the Lord's deity and the truth of His Word, you can know that you are hearing a false witness the devil has scoured up.

Perjury

Satan is in the business of lying. He's the father of the whole filthy business, and he has a lot of children who are just like their daddy. Who are these children of Satan?

Well, the perjurer is one of the devil's kids. Whoever appears in a courtroom and tells a lie is breaking the Ninth Commandment. Exodus 23:1-2 says, "Thou shalt not raise a false report: put not thine hand with the wicked to be an unrighteous witness. Thou shalt not follow a multitude to do evil."

It doesn't matter what people think. Truth is not decided by the vote of a multitude—or the vote of a jury, for that matter. Your calling from God is to speak the truth. If you perjure yourself in a courtroom, one day you will answer for that in God's courtroom. The one who accuses the innocent will suffer the penalty that the innocent person suffered. The perjurer is the child of his or her father, the devil.

Spreading Rumors

The one who spreads rumors is another of the devil's slanderous kids. The charge the false witnesses brought against Jesus was that He "said" He was going to destroy the temple in Jerusalem (Matthew 26:61).

Notice the word "said." We know from John 2:19-21 that Jesus was speaking of "the temple of his body." He was prophesying His own resurrection. But these people weren't interested in the truth. What they reported was merely a rumor that had not one syllable of truth in it.

The trouble with rumors is that they spread so much faster than the truth. D. L. Moody once said that a rumor could travel halfway around the world before the truth could get its boots on. Have you ever wondered why rumors are so popular, so readily listened to and spread by so many people? It's another evidence that the slanderer is still at work.

If you are one who is given to receiving and spreading rumors, you need to know that you are courting the discipline of Almighty God.

Going back to Exodus 23:1, notice two things. First, God forbids you from starting a rumor. Don't "*raise* a false report." You are also forbidden from having a hand in passing on a rumor. "Put not thine hand with the wicked" to keep a rumor alive by keeping it in circulation. Choke it off at its source.

Rumors are like the premature report of the death of the great American writer, Mark Twain. When Twain was in London, word somehow got back to a newspaper editor in New York that Twain either had already died or was about to die.

The editor cabled his London correspondent to check on the truth of this rumor, which would be front-page news if true. It turned out that a cousin of Twain's in London had been seriously ill but had recovered. Twain sent the editor a message that ended with the terse statement, "Report of my death greatly exaggerated."[2]

That's what rumors are—great exaggerations. In Twain's case, the rumor led to some harmless humor. But in many cases rumors can lead to great harm, even to someone's death. Look what a rumor did to the Son of God. The apostle Paul's final appeal to the church at Corinth was to repent of their sins, so that when he came there would not be "whisperings" and other sins of the tongue and heart (2 Corinthians 12:19-20).

Flattery

The perjurer breaks the Ninth Commandment. The rumormonger breaks it. And so does the flatterer. Did you know that flattery is forbidden in the Word of God? Proverbs 26:28 says, "A lying tongue hateth those that are afflicted by it; and a flattering mouth worketh ruin."

I'm not talking here about giving encouragement. You ought to give encouragement. I'm not talking about giving thanks. You ought to give thanks. I'm not talking about giving honor where honor is due. Encouragement, thanksgiving, and honor are oil that lubricate life. If somebody has done a good job, say so. Encourage people if they need uplifting.

But flattery neither encourages nor honors people. It is a way of using people. Psalm 55:21 is a classic picture of the flatterer—"The words of his mouth were smoother than butter, but war was in his heart." Have you ever met people like this? Oh, they flatter you to your face, but it's amazing what they say about you behind your back.

Do you know why a flatterer and a hypocrite are so much alike? A flatterer will say to your face what he will not say behind your back. A hypocrite will say behind your back what he will not say to your face. They are heads and tails of the same evil coin—and God's Word forbids both.

Insinuation

You can break the Ninth Commandment by mere insinuation. On one occasion when Jesus Christ was teaching, the Pharisees insinuated that He was an illegitimate child. This is the context, by the way, in which Jesus spoke the verse we read above, John 8:44. The comment that sparked His denunciation was made in verse 41, where the Pharisees said, "We be not born of fornication." The implication was Jesus *was* a product of fornication. What a horrible insinuation! It was a lie.

You can bear false witness by insinuation, by the tone of your voice, even by the arching of your eyebrows. You can also bear false witness by what you don't say.

I will never forget an incident that happened when I was a young preacher. I was driving down to my little country church with only one headlight working on my car, hoping I could wait until I got back to school to get it fixed.

But a highway patrolman stopped me. "Son, do you know you only have one headlight?"

I said, "I only have one headlight?" Now I told that officer the absolute truth. I did have only one headlight. But I said it in a way that insinuated I didn't know it before. I acted like it was a surprise.

The officer must have bought my line because he just said, "Get that thing fixed, young man." I assured him I would.

When I got back in the car, the Holy Spirit tore me up. He convicted me of lying to that patrolmen. I tried to argue with the Spirit that I didn't lie, that all I did was tell the truth. But it didn't work. The Holy Spirit convicted me of lying by insinuation.

Refusing the Lie

Refusing to bear false witness is especially important among the family of God. The Bible says in James 4:11, "Speak not evil one of another, brethren." Notice that James doesn't say it's permissible to speak evil of a brother or sister when the evil report is true. We are not to "smite" a fellow believer with our tongue (see Jeremiah 18:18).

When you listen to a falsehood, you're as liable as the false witness who gives it. It's no compliment to you that people want to use your ears for garbage cans. In some cases, you can even break the spirit of the Ninth Commandment by simply being silent, by not speaking up to affirm truth or to stop a lie.

When the Bible says you are not to bear false witness, it implies that you are to bear true witness. If you're quiet when you ought to speak, you have sinned (Leviticus 5:1). If you say, "It's none of my business" and keep silent when a criminal deed is done or a good person is slandered, you break the spirit of this Commandment.

There are few things you could do that are more foolish and more hurtful than to bear false witness. Impress this on your children, for their sake. Show them what the Word of God says about the liar and the slanderer. People say you aren't supposed to frighten children into obedience, but I say that you and your children, and I and my children, need to fear the judgment of God against the liar and to determine to stay off that path.

Proverbs 6:16-19 gives us a very important list: "These six things doth the LORD hate: yea, seven are an abomination unto him." Read that list, and you'll find that two of the seven abominations God hates deal with breaking the Ninth Commandment: "a lying tongue" (verse 17) and "a false witness that speaketh lies" (verse 19).

You may think it's a small thing to lie, but if you have a practice of lying I want to tell you very plainly that you are of your father the devil and you will spend all eternity with him in hell. Jesus said that hell was "prepared for the devil and his angels" (Matthew 25:41). The word *angel* means "messenger" or "witness." When you lie you become a witness for Satan. You become one of his angels, one of his messengers. And the Bible says in Revelation 21:8 that all liars "shall have their part in the lake which burneth with fire and brimstone."

That's the Word of God. From the lightnings and thunders of Sinai God says, "Thou shalt not bear false witness." We must recognize and respect God's truth, and we must recognize and fear the consequences of bearing false witness.

THE RELIABILITY OF A FAITHFUL WITNESS

Now that we know how God views those who bear false witness, I want to introduce you to a faithful witness and show you what it means to be a person who not only believes the truth but who lives it.

The faithful witness I want you to meet is the Old Testament prophet Micaiah. If you want an example your children can model themselves after, here it is. If you want a hero to hold up to your teenagers as you teach them to stand for the truth, Micaiah is your man.

He lived in the days of wicked King Ahab of Israel (the husband of the infamous Jezebel) and Jehoshaphat, the good king of Judah. Let's review the story as found in 1 Kings 22 and then draw five principles concerning what it takes to be a faithful witness and stand for the truth:

> And they [Ahab and Jehoshaphat] continued three years without war between Syria and Israel. And it came to pass in the third year, that Jehoshaphat the king of Judah came down to the king of Israel. And the king of Israel said unto his servants, Know ye that Ramoth in Gilead is ours, and we be still, and take it not out of the hand of the king of Syria? And he said unto Jehoshaphat, Wilt thou go with me to battle to Ramoth-gilead? And

Jehoshaphat said to the king of Israel, I am as thou art, my people as thy people, my horses as thy horses.

—Verses 1-4

As I noted above, Jehoshaphat was a good king, but he got in serious trouble because he couldn't face the truth. As the story progressed, he failed to rely on the only faithful witness in Ahab's entire court, the prophet Micaiah.

Ahab and Jehoshaphat made their battle plans and *then* decided to consult the Lord. Now that's backwards, so they were in trouble already. When Jehoshaphat asked Ahab to seek a word from the Lord, Ahab called together his 400 pandering, pussy-footing prophets, who rubber-stamped the decision he had already made. "Go up," they all said, "for the LORD shall deliver it into the hand of the king" (verses 5-6).

Jehoshaphat must have been a little skeptical about 400 preachers agreeing so completely on something. So he asked Ahab, "Is there not here a prophet of the LORD besides, that we might inquire of him?" (verse 7). Ahab said there was one more, Micaiah, number 401: "But I hate him; for he doth not prophesy good concerning me, but evil" (verse 8). Nevertheless, they sent for Micaiah. The messenger who came to get him warned him that all of Ahab's prophets had already prophesied success, so Micaiah had better be sure just to add his own word of blessing (verse 13).

Now here's the verse I want to burn into your soul and mine, and into the souls of your children: "And Micaiah said, As the LORD liveth, what the LORD saith unto me, that will I speak" (verse 14). You can read 1 Kings 22:15-40 to find out what happened after that. You'll see that after mocking Ahab a bit with the answer he wanted, Micaiah correctly prophesied that Ahab's military campaign was doomed to disaster by the Lord and that it would cost Ahab his life. Micaiah's reward for telling the truth was a punch in the face and a stint in prison. But all things happened just as Micaiah had prophesied.

This is such a powerful example of what it takes to be a faithful witness that I want to share with you five principles that will help you and your children be truthful witnesses as the Ninth Commandment requires.

1. It is better to be divided by truth than united in error.

This is the first thing we learn from Micaiah's life. I love unity. The Bible loves unity. We are to keep the unity of the Spirit (Ephesians 4:3). But Amos 3:3 asks a pertinent question: "Can two walk together, except they be agreed?" Don't sacrifice the truth on the altar of unity. There are no cooks in the world skilled enough to make a good omelette out of bad eggs. Unity in the truth? Yes. But unification and uniformity where truth is sacrificed? Never.

2. It is better to tell the truth that hurts and then heals
than to tell a lie that comforts and then kills.

Four hundred prophets told King Ahab of Israel a lie that comforted him in the short run but eventually killed him. I imagine he was so happy with the prophecy of victory from those false prophets that they probably had their picture taken with the king right afterwards.

But there was one prophet, Micaiah, who refused to give Ahab false comfort. The sad thing is that Ahab hated the message that would have saved his life, and he hated the messenger who delivered it. My late predecessor, Dr. Robert G. Lee, once said, "It is better to be called cruel for being kind than to be called kind for being cruel." Rough truth is better than polished falsehood (see Ecclesiastes 5:7; Proverbs 27:5-6).

3. It is better to be hated for telling the truth than to be
loved for telling a lie.

Ahab said of Micaiah, "I hate him." The apostle Paul told the Galatians the truth, and then he had to ask them, "Am I therefore become your enemy, because I tell you the truth?" (Galatians 4:16).

You need to help your children understand that if they tell the truth, they may not get elected "most popular" at school. Children are often thrown for a big loss by this because they tend to judge things in terms of what's fair, and this world is seldom fair. But if they tell the truth and suffer for it, they are in good company. The Lord Jesus told the truth, and His enemies crucified Him for it (see John 7:7).

4. It is better to stand alone with the truth than to be
wrong with a multitude.

Four hundred to one was pretty heavy odds. But that's what Micaiah faced. We need to remember that the majority is frequently wrong. Every one of those faithless preachers in Ahab's court was wrong.

Think of Noah, who preached with the wrath of God in the fore-ground and the ring of hammers in the background. Noah and his family stood alone and went into the ark a minority. But they came out a majority!

Don't think that the example of Micaiah is far removed from you and your children. You may be called on to stand alone for truth just as he was. Your children may have to stand alone for truth in their classrooms. We need to arm ourselves with the truth and prepare our children to stand for it.

  5. *It is better to ultimately succeed with the truth than to temporarily*
     succeed with a lie.

Ahab went into battle, and God's arrow found him. But God's crown found Micaiah. We need to stay with the Word of God because it is the only thing that will stand the test of time and ultimately succeed.

I like what former President Woodrow Wilson said—"I would rather temporarily fail with a cause that will ultimately succeed, than to temporarily succeed with a cause that will ultimately fail."

Do you want to be a faithful witness to the truth and raise children who will stand for the truth in their generation? Then say like Micaiah, "As the LORD liveth, what the LORD saith unto me, that will I speak."

THE RESPONSIBILITY OF A FAMILY WITNESS

There is a crying need in America today for families that know the truth, believe the truth, love the truth, teach the truth, speak the truth, and share the truth. A home that is not built on truth will crumble.

How do we take these things we have talked about and teach them to our children, so that they might go out to the school, to the workplace, and to the government and permeate society with truth? Let me give you three basic ways.

Teaching by Precept

We can teach them by precept. Get out God's Word, and show your children what it says about telling the truth. Teach them God's precepts. Show your kids that when they tell a lie, they're acting like the devil. And be sure to show them that when they tell the truth, they're acting like the Lord Jesus Christ.

Don't just say, "Don't lie." Give them the biblical reasons. Tell your children why they ought to tell the truth. Make certain your children understand God's holy Commandments.

Teaching by Example

Be a godly example in this area. I cannot say it well enough or strongly enough: Dad, be a father who tells the truth. One of the grandest things that has happened in America today is a movement called Promise Keepers, which is calling men to keep their promises to their families and to God.

Both fathers and mothers need to be able to say to their children, "God says we are not to lie. As He is my witness and my helper, I will never lie to you. I will always keep my word to you." You can fail in many ways and still come out on the plus side with your children. But if you fail to keep your word, if you fail to tell your children the truth, I promise you that your home is on the road to disaster.

I cannot emphasize enough how important it is to have fathers who tell the truth. Christian father, if you have ever made a promise to your child and failed to keep it, ask that child for forgiveness.

One day I got all of my children together and asked them, "Have I ever promised you anything that I didn't do?" I was sure they'd say, "Oh no, Dad. You've always kept your word." But one of them surprised me by reminding me of a time when I'd made an offhand remark that was taken as a promise. You know how we parents will sometimes say, "One of these days we'll do this or that." So I asked for my child's forgiveness.

Don't be afraid to admit it when you've done wrong. Let your children know that you are a truth-speaker.

Now, Dad, I'm going to meddle a little. Do you have one of these little boxes they call "fuzz busters" in your car? Why do you have it there? Or better yet, why do your children think you have it there? If you have it because you sometimes absentmindedly go over the speed limit and you want to be reminded so you will stay within the law, tell your children so. But if it's there to help you "beat the system," your family will soon know it, and you should get rid of it.

I mention this because for most of us it's often the little daily things that catch us when it comes to truth-telling. For instance, what do you do when little Throckmorton has just turned twelve and you go to a family movie? If Throckmorton were under twelve, you could save a few bucks. And besides, he's only been twelve for a couple of days. Do you say, "Well, just tell them you're under twelve, son. No harm done"? You will rue the day you do that.

I remember when we took our family to an amusement park in Fort Lauderdale, Florida. You know how expensive those places are when you have four kids, as Joyce and I did then.

We got to the window, and I counted my money and discovered we were something like seventy-five cents short of having enough to get all of us into the park. And the park wouldn't take a check. The children were heartbroken. We were standing there trying to figure out what to do when we saw that the price for twelve-and-under children was reduced. My oldest had just turned twelve a few days before.

He said, "Daddy, I just turned twelve. We could just say I'm under twelve so we can get in." The Rogers family had a moral crisis on its hands.

I said, "I'm sorry, son. We just can't do that. It would be a lie." I won't bother you with the rest of the story, but God intervened and we all got in that day without breaking the rules. It was a great lesson for all of us.

Do your children know that you tell the truth? Do you teach your children to pick up the phone for you and say, "Mama's not here" when you are? If we teach them to lie *for* us, we should never punish them when they lie *to* us.

Teach your children by precept. Show them from the Bible why they should not lie. I heard about a mother who told her son, "Johnny, if you don't stop lying, there's a green man that lives on the moon who's going to catch you and make you pick up sticks the rest of your life." We don't need to make up stories to scare our sons and daughters into being truthful. Teach them the Word.

Teach your children by example. Live the Word of God in your home. Tell the truth to your children, and keep your word.

Teaching by Discipline

Teach these truths by discipline. There were three deadly D's our kids knew about when they were growing up, three things they knew their parents would not put up with.

The first is deliberate disobedience. A child can disobey in a way that is not arrogant or deliberate. In those cases, you have to deal gently with the child. But when it is deliberate disobedience, you must deal with that immediately and decisively.

The second deadly D is defiance. That's disobedience with a disrespectful attitude—a defiant disrespect for parental authority or any authority, for that matter.

The third is dishonesty. If the Ninth Commandment means anything, it means that we cannot let our children get away with lying. God's judgment is sure on those who bear false witness. We can spare our children God's discipline by dealing immediately, kindly, and yet sternly with dishonesty.

If we want our homes to be successful, we must go back to God's blueprint for the home. We must lay the foundation of God's holy Commandments. Take the Ten Commandments one at a time; measure your own life by them, and teach them to your children. You'll be blessed when you do.

TURNING THE COMMANDMENTS INTO COMMITMENTS

0-6 Years

- Establish firm penalties for lying, and don't let a lie pass without dealing with it.

- Reward truth-telling with sincere appreciation.

- Gather stories, music, and videos that underscore the importance of telling the truth.

- Try to avoid using exaggeration with your little ones, and help them not to exaggerate.

7-12 Years

- Look for situations in the news and in your own world that can serve as the basis for a dinnertime discussion about lying.

- Ask your kids for examples from school of those who either told the truth or lied. Ask them what happened as a result.

- Don't make promises you can't keep.

13+ Years

- Promise yourself that you and your mate will not cover for your children if they are caught lying.

- Reward truthfulness above just about anything else your teens do right.

- Help them deal with the reality that the world does not always reward the truth.

11

THE SECRET OF SATISFACTION

To whom little is not enough, nothing is enough.

—Anonymous

D o you know the last of God's Ten Commandments? This is what
it says:

> Thou shalt not covet thy neighbor's house, thou shalt not covet
> thy neighbor's wife, nor his manservant, nor his maidservant,
> nor his ox, nor his ass, nor any thing that is thy neighbor's.
>
> *—Exodus 20:17*

The advertising boys on Madison Avenue have done a good job of
giving us all a bad case of the "wants." We have been told that we cannot be happy unless we have something else that's newer, bigger, better,
and shinier than what we already have. And the advertisers have done
an even better job of convincing our children that they simply must have
the last thing they saw on television.

It is advertisers' job to create perceived needs in us so we will go out
and buy what they're selling. We're told we deserve it and that these
things will make us happy. But the truth of the matter is, this desire for
more and more is making us unhappy.

Surveys of married couples reveal that the primary cause of marital unhappiness and unhappiness in the homes is not sex, nor children or in-laws, but possessions and attitudes toward money. Couples who get married today expect to have in three years what their parents accumulated in thirty years, and they get it with the false god of credit.

Of course, they pay the debt not with their checkbook, but too often with their marriage. "'Till debt do us part" becomes their vow because they have not learned to live without certain things. They're not content.

How many truly contented people do you know? We never seem to get enough stuff. The quotation at the beginning of this chapter says a lot about the problem of coveting. Once you give in to it, you are never really satisfied.

The Bible says not to covet. What does that mean? To covet means to have an unlawful desire for that which is not rightfully yours. Covetousness is not limited to money. It could involve influence, fame, power, or appearance. You must not covet your neighbor's salary. Don't covet his education. Don't covet his advantages. Don't covet anything that belongs to your neighbor.

The Tenth Commandment is not a command against lawful desire. When God saves you, He doesn't neuter you. He doesn't make you a person without passion. It's not wrong to have godly ambition.

It's not necessarily wrong to desire things. The Bible says it is the Lord "that giveth thee power to get wealth" (Deuteronomy 8:18). "Every good gift and every perfect gift is from above, and cometh down from the Father of lights, with whom is no variableness, neither shadow of turning" (James 1:17).

God knows you want to love and be loved. You have a God-given desire for friendship and a home, for happiness, joy, success, victory, peace. These things are not wrong. They are from God. It is the *unlawful* desire that we're going to be talking about. The Bible calls this covetousness, the subject of the last Commandment in this chain of ten links.

Why is it the last one? Because it sums up all of the others. The other Commandments deal with actions, but this one deals with attitude. The others deal with needs, but this one deals with desire. This Commandment deals with the heart, because until we've dealt with the heart, the rest of the Commandments are only rules we'll find impossible to obey.

A Perplexing Problem

The first thing I want you to notice as we consider the secret of satisfaction is the perplexing problem of covetousness. Do you know why it's such a big problem? Here are a few reasons.

A Deceitful Thing

Covetousness is terribly deceitful. Very few people even realize they are covetous because we become so used to it. Charles Haddon Spurgeon, the great preacher of yesteryear, said, "I've seen thousands of people converted, but I've never seen a covetous person converted."

Obviously covetous people do get converted. Spurgeon was saying that tongue-in-cheek. What he meant was he had never heard anybody say, "You know, my problem before I got saved was covetousness." The great Catholic theologian Francis Xavier once said, "I have listened to multiplied thousands of confessions. I've yet to have one person ever confess the sin of covetousness."

Isn't that amazing? That's why the Bible speaks of the "cloak of covetousness" (1 Thessalonians 2:5). Covetousness is something that none of us thinks he has. We think the other person has it. But until we get to the root of the problem we'll never get to a solution.

The apostle Paul was once a young Pharisee—praised, admired, looked up to. He seemed to have it all. He had prestigious birth. He had nobility. He had education. He had status. He had learning. He had respect.

One day this proud young Pharisee was taking a self-survey. He had the Ten Commandments out and was checking them off. "Let's see—'Thou shalt have no other gods before me.' Check. I serve Jehovah only. 'Thou shalt not make unto thee any graven image.' Why, I certainly wouldn't do that. I'm not an idolater. 'Thou shalt not take the name of the LORD thy God in vain.' Never! 'Remember the sabbath day, to keep it holy.' I always do."

Paul went right down the list. He was doing fine—until he got to the tenth and last Commandment: "Thou shalt not covet." Now he was in trouble. Read what he said about it in Romans 7:7—"I had not known sin, but by the law: for I had not known lust, except the law had said, Thou shalt not covet."

Paul said that Commandment wiped him out. It knocked the props out from under him, because while he might say he had never done those other things, he couldn't say he never wanted to.

Paul was saying that the unlawful desire in his heart made him know he was a sinner before a righteous and holy God. That's the way he knew sin, by this Tenth Commandment that told him not to covet.

You know, sometimes you can hold things in pretty well. I heard about a preacher who was playing golf with some businessmen. They were a pretty rough bunch, using language I sometimes hear on the golf course when that little orb doesn't go just right. The preacher made some pretty bad shots himself, but he seemed to keep his composure.

One of the men said to him, "Preacher, I admire you. You've got it all together. You never say any of those bad words like the rest of us."

The preacher replied, "Well, let me be very honest with you. If you'll notice, where I spit, the grass never grows again."

Sometimes we can hold sinful desires in so they don't come to the surface. But inside, in our heart . . . Maybe you don't take God's name in vain, but you want to. Maybe you didn't commit adultery, but did you ever desire to? Maybe you didn't steal, but are you ever tempted? Maybe you didn't kill, but have you wanted to? Questions like these bring us up short, because they make us realize what a deceitful thing covetousness is.

A Debasing Thing

Covetousness is also a very debasing thing. Nothing shows our depravity more than our covetousness. Mark 7:21 is God's X-ray of the human heart. There Jesus said, "For from within, out of the heart of men, proceed evil thoughts, adulteries, fornications, murders."

A man is not an adulterer because he commits adultery. He commits adultery because he's an adulterer. A man is not a thief because he steals. He steals because he's a thief. A man is not a liar because he tells lies. He tells lies because he's a liar. These things come out of the heart.

Notice verses 22-23 of Mark 7—"thefts, covetousness, wickedness, deceit, lasciviousness, an evil eye, blasphemy, pride, foolishness: all these evil things come from within, and defile the man."

Covetousness was born in you. You were born with a sin nature that you received from your spiritual father, the devil. Jesus said to the unsaved, "Ye are of your father the devil, and the lusts of your father ye will do" (John 8:44).

The high-ranking angel Lucifer coveted the throne of God. He became the devil by wanting what was not his. He said, "I will exalt my throne above the stars of God. . . . I will be like the Most High" (Isaiah 14:13-14). That, in plain language, is covetousness.

Then, in the Garden of Eden, the devil tempted Adam and Eve to covet the same thing, being like God (Genesis 3:5). All of us are born with that sinful nature because of the sin of Adam and because of the nature we inherit from him.

How does this work? Well, here's two-year-old Throckmorton, playing happily on the floor, surrounded by about fifteen toys. His mother has a guest come over and bring her little boy Alphonso with her, so the two boys can play while the mothers talk and have a cup of tea.

Little Alphonso's mother sets him down next to little Throckmorton, and he picks up a toy. Throckmorton still has fourteen toys. But when he sees that Alphonso has just one, Throckmorton leaves his fourteen toys and goes over and bops Alphonso on the head to take that one toy back. Sound familiar? That's the way children are.

Little children are naturally selfish. Their first instinct is to hold on to what they get. That's human nature. That's kind of humorous when it's a child, but when Throckmorton gets to be a grown man, it won't be very funny.

Covetousness is a very debasing thing. It's an octopus that wraps itself around your soul. And the trouble with a covetous person is that he not only poisons his own life with misery, but he spoils everyone and everything else he touches. The self-centered person is of all people most miserable. But that's the way we are by nature. The Bible calls it covetousness.

Lest you think the solution to the sin of covetousness is education, let me disabuse you of that mistaken notion. Survey after survey of the best and brightest among college students reveals that for countless numbers of young people things like wealth, power, fame, and ambition are at the top of their list of desires. These students want the finest and biggest.

That should not surprise those of us who believe the Bible. And I'm not trying to be hard on college students, because their desires are simply a reflection of the covetousness that is in all human hearts by nature. All of us carry its seed within us.

That is why the Bible deals so sternly with coveting, and why we must do so as well. If your children are not taught how not to yield to this sin, a lot of other lessons you try to teach them will be lost.

As in the case of every other Commandment we have talked about, teaching your children about greed starts with your own attitude. If you want to see how you're doing with the Tenth Commandment and where your heart really is, add up everything you value highly that money can't buy or that debt—or death—can't take away. What you have when all the material stuff is stripped away will tell you who you really are.

A Destructive Thing

Covetousness is deceptive. It is depraving. And it is terribly destructive. It will annihilate you. Consider 1 Timothy 6:6-10:

> But godliness with contentment is great gain. For we brought nothing into this world, and it is certain we can carry nothing out. And having food and raiment, let us be therewith content. But they that will be rich fall into temptation and a snare, and into many foolish and hurtful lusts, which drown men in destruction and perdition. For the love of money is the root of all evil: which while some coveted after, they have erred from the faith, and pierced themselves through with many sorrows.

The key here is the phrase, "they that will be rich." That means desire, a dogged determination to get rich. But the very thing some people desire does not bring them joy or peace. It afflicts them with many sorrows. You don't have to look far to see that demonstrated today. You could say the love of money is the mother of all sins. It is the root of all kinds of evil.

Never ever tell your child, "Sweetheart, make all the money you can, just so you make it honestly." That's often what you hear at college graduation exercises.

But wait a minute. If you're making all the money you can, then you're making money when you ought to be sleeping. You're making money when you ought to be spending time with your family. You're making money when you ought to be fishing. You're making money when you ought to be soul-winning, praying, attending church. If you have a consuming desire to be rich, everything else must go.

"No servant can serve two masters," Jesus said (Luke 16:13). He said, "Seek ye first the kingdom of God, and his righteousness; and all these things shall be added unto you" (Matthew 6:33). Either God is first, or mammon (money) is first. You cannot serve both. When you say, "I want to be rich no matter what," you have set up an idol of covetousness in your heart that causes you to break all of the other nine Commandments.

For example, the first two Commandments deal with having no other gods. They forbid idolatry. But the Bible calls covetousness idolatry (Colossians 3:5). So when you covet, you've broken the first two Commandments.

The Third Commandment says not to take God's name in vain. But how often do people who claim to be Christians misuse and abuse the name of God as they seek after wealth?

"Remember the sabbath day, to keep it holy," says the Fourth Commandment. But rather than working six days and resting one, we work seven days. Why? Covetousness. Why do people steal? Covetousness. Why do people lie? Covetousness. Why do people commit adultery? They covet somebody else's wife.

All of the Ten Commandments are broken when we have a spirit of covetousness. This sin is incredibly destructive. That's the reason the Bible says the love of money is the root of all kinds of evil. When you have covetousness in your heart, when you have this unlawful desire, your life is bent and broken and you destroy others. As I said above, covetousness is an octopus that will wrap itself around your soul and literally drag you into hell.

Does that sound too harsh? Just listen to the apostle Paul in Ephesians 5:5:

> For this ye know, that no whoremonger, nor unclean person, nor covetous man, who is an idolater, hath any inheritance in the kingdom of Christ and of God.

God links covetousness with whoremongering, perversion, and idolatry. Don't think this is a small sin. It is the root of all the rest of them.

A PROPER PERSPECTIVE

Since covetousness is such a perplexing problem, how do we deal with it? We've got to back off and get a proper perspective on the whole thing. We need to understand who we are and what we have, especially as we think about how to teach our children the truth of the Tenth Commandment.

Hebrews 13:5 is a good place to start. Here is the secret of satisfaction and the answer to covetousness: "Let your conversation [your lifestyle] be without covetousness; and be content with such things as ye have: for he [God] hath said, I will never leave thee, nor forsake thee."

That's just a restatement of the Tenth Commandment. You will always be covetous until you learn contentment. Why? Because all of us need satisfaction, and covetousness in essence means trying to find satisfaction in the wrong place. The secret of satisfaction is to be content with what you have.

What You Have

The question is, what do you really have? The brilliant author Ernest Hemingway died of suicide because despite his wealth and celebrity he considered life to be "just a dirty trick, a short journey from nothingness to nothingness."

To Hemingway, life didn't make sense. It was a joke, and a bad joke at that. Think about the man who doesn't know God. He gets everything he wants, and there's still a hole in his soul. All he can look forward to is a hole in the ground, a place to rot and decay. There's no answer. There's no meaning.

It's a shame Ernest Hemingway didn't know Jesus. It's a shame he did not find satisfaction and joy and meaning in the Lord Jesus Christ. Hemingway didn't have the proper perspective on life.

What do you have? If you're a child of God, twice-born and blood-bought, a member of His family, you have abundance.

You have God Himself. You have Him, and He has you. The psalmist said, "Whom have I in heaven but thee? And there is none upon earth that I desire besides thee. My flesh and my heart faileth: but God is the strength of my heart, and my portion for ever" (Psalm 73:25-26).

You have your family. "Whoso findeth a wife findeth a good thing" (Proverbs 18:22). "Lo, children are a heritage of the LORD" (Psalm 127:3). If you have children, count your blessings. Thank God for them.

There are people today who don't want to have children because they want things—material possessions or pleasures—instead. They say, "Children make a rich man poor." No, they've got it backward. Children make a poor man rich. A rich man can't take his riches to heaven, but I'm taking my children to heaven. Thank God for your children. They are a heritage from the Lord.

J. Paul Getty was one of the richest men who ever lived. You wouldn't expect him to be envious of anyone. But Getty once said he was envious of those who knew how to make marriage work and to be happy in marriage. Getty knew whereof he spoke, because his record was five marriages and five divorces. If you have a happy home, you're rich. You're blessed.

You have friends. "A friend loveth at all times" (Proverbs 17:17). During the morning worship services at our church, the other men on the platform and I get together and speak a word to each other. One morning one of the men put his arms around me and said, "I love you." It's wonderful to be loved and to know it! If you have friends, you are a wealthy person.

You have God's wisdom. If you have discovered the treasure trove of godly wisdom, how rich you are:

> Happy is the man that findeth wisdom, and the man that getteth understanding: for the merchandise of it is better than the merchandise of silver, and the gain thereof than fine gold.
> —Proverbs 3:13-14

I would not trade my knowledge of the Bible for all of the money, the rubies, the diamonds, the gold and silver this world has. There are millions of people sitting in darkness who would leap for joy to know what you know, to have the wisdom of God's Word. It's better than silver or gold.

You have satisfaction. Can you say like Paul that you have learned to be content in all kinds of circumstances (Philippians 4:11-12)? Can you say not only that Jesus is necessary, but that He's enough? If you can say that, you can be satisfied. I am satisfied with Jesus. I am not satisfied with my Christian life, but I have the peace that passes understanding in the Lord Jesus Christ.

What You Need

I was once witnessing to a man as we stood in front of his house. I couldn't get very far with him. He was seemingly very satisfied. He said, "I've got a good income. I don't owe anybody anything. I own my house. I own my car. My wife loves me."

He didn't say it, but he reminded me of the church at Laodicea (Revelation 3:17), where the people said they were rich and needed nothing.

I said, "All right. But I want to ask you a question. Will you be honest with me?"

He said, "Sure."

"Now don't just say it," I replied. "Will you be absolutely honest with me?" I knew I had him, because he was a man who prided himself on his honesty.

"Yes, I will."

"All right. Do you have peace in your heart?"

He said, "I told you I had all these things."

"No, I'm not talking about all that," I answered. "Do you have peace in your heart?"

His chin started to quiver, and his eyes brimmed with tears as he answered, "No, I don't have peace in my heart. How did you know?"

"Because the Bible says there is no peace to the wicked—those who have not come to God. These things that you have cannot fill the longing in your heart. You need Jesus."

If you have Jesus, you have the peace of God that passes all understanding. If you have that, you are a rich person. But if you don't have Jesus, you need Him more than you have ever needed anything in your life.

John Muir was a great naturalist in the early part of this century. He was largely responsible for the creation of Yellowstone National Park and the formation of conservation policy in this country.

Muir lived a very simple life, and yet he once said that he was wealthier than railroad magnate E. H. Harriman, who had acquired millions of dollars. When asked how he could say this, Muir replied, "Because I have all the money I want, and he hasn't."[1] You see, to whom little is not enough, nothing is enough.

What you need is a proper perspective on this matter of covetousness. Understand who you are. Let your life be free of it. God has said He will never leave or forsake you. What more do you need?

THE PRACTICE OF SATISFACTION

Now that we have considered the problem of covetousness and looked at it from a proper perspective, let's talk about the practice of satisfaction. Let me give you some ideas to help you teach your children how to keep the Tenth Commandment.

Give Your Heart to Christ

We've already alluded to this. Give your heart to the Lord. Find your satisfaction in Him. Let Him meet the deepest needs of your heart; turn your eyes upon Him. God has so engineered you that this world will not satisfy you.

We were made for God, and it's only in Him that "we live, and move, and have our being" (Acts 17:27). You'll never deal with covetousness unless you give all you know of you to all you know of Him. Let go of this world with both hands, and take hold of Him with both hands.

Cultivate Gratitude

Demonstrate before your children a spirit of gratitude, and cultivate that spirit in them. Be thankful for what you have. Review with your children the ways God has helped and prospered you spiritually. Keep a family scrapbook of God's provisions and the ways He has answered your prayers and heart desires. Let your children know how rich you are through Christ. Think and talk often of your blessings.

Why would a teenager with a closet full of clothes say, "I don't have anything to wear"? Why would kids with Nintendo and all those computer games and all the latest toys say, "I'm bored"? Why would adults with all of their things to enhance life say, "I just don't feel good about myself"?

What's wrong? We have failed to be grateful. We have failed to see what God has given us. Don't fall into that trap.

Learn to Love

If you're a covetous person, you might love things, but you don't love people. Nobody can be covetous and love others. When you covet what others have, you don't really love them. If you loved them, you would rejoice in what they have. When I go into a fine home or see somebody who has nice things, I make it a practice to bow my head privately and thank God for His blessings on those people.

Every person who loves another person rejoices in what that person has. Celebrate God's grace and goodness to somebody else. Teach your children that somebody else's blessing is not your loss. For many of us, the problem is not just wanting more—it is wanting more than somebody else.

Just love those people who may have more than you. Thank God that He has blessed them. Let go of covetousness.

Know Who You Are

Understand who you are in the Lord Jesus Christ. Teach your children that they are saints, that they have the righteousness of God in Jesus Christ. Teach them to get their identity not from Madison Avenue, but from the Word of God. Help them celebrate their distinctiveness and their differences.

Learn to Give

I don't know of anything that will kill covetousness more quickly than learning to give. A pastor friend of mine was talking to a U.S. Congressman, who told him, "Pastor, I want to tell you what God has taught me about giving. I took my son to McDonald's. He wanted some french fries, so I bought him a large order and we sat down for some father and son fellowship. As we sat at the table, I got to smelling those fries. I thought I would have a couple, so I reached over and started to take some. But my son put his hand on mine and said, 'Hey, those are mine.' That just went right through me. I thought, 'My son has a bad attitude.'

"But in a moment, in less time than it takes to tell it, God spoke to my heart and gave me one of the greatest lessons about stewardship I have ever learned."

Here is what the Congressman learned. He said, "I thought three things about my son. Number one, he'd evidently forgotten where those french fries came from. I'm the one who bought them. Number two, he doesn't understand that I have the power to take them all away from him. Or if I wanted to, I could go buy twenty more large orders and bury him in french fries. Number three, my son didn't realize that if I wanted more fries for myself, I've got the money to go up and buy them and sit at another table and eat them all by myself. My son has an attitude problem.

"But then God spoke to me and said, 'That's exactly the attitude you have sometimes. You need to remember where your blessings come from. I'm the one who gave you these things. And you need to understand that I have the power to take them away from you or to give you more. And you need to understand that I don't need what you have. I can have my own.'"

That's a powerful lesson. God doesn't need us; we need Him. Nothing will dynamite the covetousness out of our hearts like learning to give to God and to others. Teach your children to give, show them how to give, and you'll add another brick to the building of a successful home.

THE REAL PROBLEM

Our real problem is not that we break the Ten Commandments. That's only a symptom. The real problem is our hearts. We need to be saved. We need to be born again, because keeping the Ten Commandments won't get anybody to heaven. You have to be saved by receiving Jesus

Christ as your Lord and Savior. Then He will give you the power to live as you ought to live.

If you have never trusted Jesus as your Savior, or if you're not sure of your standing before Him, I invite you to pray this simple prayer right now:

> Jesus, You died to save me, and You promised to save me if I would trust You. I do trust You, Lord Jesus. I believe You're the Son of God. I believe You paid my sin-debt with Your blood on the cross. I believe that God raised You from the dead. And now by faith I receive You into my life as my Lord and Savior. I'm sorry for my sin. I turn from my sin. Forgive me. Cleanse me. Come into my life, and begin now to make me the person You want me to be. Amen.

If you know Jesus, then you know that the secret of satisfaction isn't found in anything on earth. It's found only in Him!

Turning the Commandments into Commitments

0-6 Years

- Encourage your children to thank Jesus when a sibling or a friend gets something new or something good happens to someone else.

- Avoid complaining about your possessions.
  Your kids will get the idea that God isn't taking very good care of you.

- If contentment is a problem for you, begin now asking God to do a new work in your heart.

7-12 Years

- Teach gratitude by insisting that your children write thank-you notes to whoever has done something for them or has given them something.

- Require your children to give to God and to others from whatever money they receive.

- Consider sponsoring a needy child as a family, and let the kids have a part in earning the money needed.

13+ Years

- Explain your giving plan to your children; show them how you give.
- Gradually turn responsibility for your kids' giving over to them; become their encourager rather than their financial manager.
- Help your teens make good choices about possessions; show them that they can't have everything they want.

12

A WORD OF ENCOURAGEMENT

Oh God, I will not stand before Thee without all of my children.

—*Catherine Booth*

We have talked about many truths in the preceding chapters. I have tried not only to help you understand and apply the truth of God to your own life, but to teach His commands and precepts to your children.

But I have been preaching God's Word and working with families long enough to know that sometimes the thought of trying to teach God's Word to their children can overwhelm some good and conscientious parents. They look at the whole scope of a project like teaching the Ten Commandments rather than taking things one step at a time, and it seems like too much to get across.

Other parents have tried family devotions or Bible times in various forms and have gotten discouraged for different reasons. So they tend to give up and say, "I just can't make it work."

Still other parents find it hard to get started teaching the Bible in their home because they are bound by guilt. It may be guilt over their own failures or guilt over mistakes they have made with their children. But whatever the cause, these parents feel unworthy to open the Word and to teach it to others.

If you fall into any of these categories—or even if you're sailing right along and having regular and wonderful family devotions—I want to offer you a strong word of biblical encouragement in our final chapter together. I want you to know and believe that God will help you teach your children, and that He will bless your efforts if you will just look to Him and lean on Him.

For your encouragement and instruction in this important process, I want to consider with you one of the most powerful principles in all of Scripture—a principle that will, if you heed it in your home, do more than just about anything else to prepare your children to be godly men and women, wise fathers and mothers, and fruitful members of the body of Christ.

My purpose in this chapter is not to overwhelm you with more information or to heap guilt upon you. By God's grace, I want to encourage, uplift, and equip you for the all-important task of raising your children to know, love, and follow Jesus Christ.

So let me give you the principle. It is stated in this very familiar, though often misunderstood, verse:

> Train up a child in the way he should go: and when he is old, he will not depart from it.
>
> —Proverbs 22:6

What wisdom the Bible packs into a few words!

This is the principle, short and sweet. Let's see what it means by considering four very valuable techniques this verse gives us for training our children.

COMMENCE IN CHILDHOOD

First of all, notice that Proverbs 22:6 says, "Train up a *child*" (my emphasis). Training is most effective when it begins in the earliest years of childhood.

The word "train" here has the idea of dedicating. This could be translated, "Dedicate a child in the way he should go." Have you dedicated your children to the Lord? When each of our children was so dedicated, Joyce and I got on our knees and gave that precious child to the

Lord Jesus Christ. In fact, we have dedicated our children to the Lord over and over again.

Why should you start training your children when they're young? Why does the Bible say, "Train up a child" rather than "Train up a young person"? There are several factors that make early training the most desirable.

The Correction Factor

The first factor is the correction factor. It is so much easier to correct children when they're young and more pliable than it is when they are older.

You can take a little trickle of a stream and steer it any way you wish. But it's hard to steer the mighty Mississippi River. You can bend a little twig in any direction you choose, but it's hard to bend a mighty oak tree.

You can correct a child, but once he gets to be a man, it's going to be very hard to change him. Proverbs 19:18 has a wise word for us parents: "Chasten thy son while there is hope."

Many parents have come to their pastor for counseling with this complaint: "Pastor, we don't know what to do with our son. He's on drugs. He's dishonest. He's into rock music. He's into this and that, and he's so rebellious we just can't handle him. What should we do?"

It's good when parents in that situation wake up and start looking for help. But the problem is, they're starting about sixteen years and 175 pounds too late. We need to teach our children God's Commandments while they are young, open, and teachable.

Proverbs 13:24 says, "He that spareth his rod hateth his son: but he that loveth him chasteneth him betimes." "Betimes" is an old *King James* word that literally means "early"—that is, when a child is young, when it's easier to correct him.

You may say, "But my children don't need correcting. They're little angels." I know they're all little angels. But let me tell you, as their legs get longer, you're going to find their wings get shorter! Your children are not little angels dropped down from heaven with halos around their heads. And neither are mine.

The Communication Factor

Here is a second factor that argues for early child training. Childhood is a wonderful time for communication. Little children have a great ability to learn. One reason for that is their great curiosity. They always want to know why.

I know a child's questions get a little wearisome at times, but don't quench that wonderful curiosity. God has built it into your child. God told the Israelites that when their children asked why they did something or what a particular memorial meant, the parents should be ready to explain it to them.

Children also have a great memory capacity. It's amazing what little ones can learn and retain. All of my grandchildren speak a foreign language. And what's more, they learned it at an incredibly early age. Which foreign language do they speak? English. I mean, they weren't born with English already programmed into their heads. They had to learn it. And English is a complicated language where there are more exceptions than rules.

But here's something even more amazing. Over in Japan there are tiny children learning Japanese! Now that's a hard language. How do little Japanese children learn that language? The same way American kids learn English.

God has given children a great capacity for learning and memorizing. Besides that, they are humble enough to be taught, and they trust what their parents tell them.

Childhood is the optimum time to communicate God's truth to your children. Tomorrow that toddler won't be asking why. Tomorrow that schoolboy won't be asking for help with his homework. And tomorrow that teenager will not want to hang around the house with his or her friends.

The Conversion Factor

Early childhood is also the best time for conversion. We ought to see to it that our children find Christ at an early age. I am tired of people playing down childhood conversions, as if it's wrong to lead a child to Christ. Where did we get the idea that a person has to have a Ph.D. in sin before he can get saved?

Now of course we shouldn't manipulate children—or anyone else, for that matter—into trusting Christ. Children don't need to be tricked or coerced into coming to Jesus. They only need to be guided. It ought to be perfectly normal and natural for children to come to know Jesus as their Savior and Lord if they're raised in a Christian home.

I love Mark 10:13-16, where some parents brought their young children to Jesus so He could touch them. Let's pick up the story at the end of verse 13:

> [But] his disciples rebuked those that brought them. But when Jesus saw it, he was much displeased, and said unto them, Suffer the little children to come unto me, and forbid them not: for of such is the kingdom of God. Verily I say unto you, Whosoever shall not receive the kingdom of God as a little child, he shall not enter therein. And he took them up in his arms, put his hands upon them, and blessed them.

You see, Jesus had just been dealing with the Pharisees over the very deep subject of divorce. So the disciples thought that Jesus was too busy with the learned doctors of religion to be bothered with little children. But He set them straight in a hurry.

We sometimes think a little child has to become like an adult to understand the things of God, but Jesus says the adult has to become like a little child. Children can be and should be saved at an early age.

The great theologian and writer Matthew Henry, whose Bible commentary many of us still use today, was saved at the age of eleven. The great American preacher and theologian Jonathan Edwards, considered by many to be the greatest mind this nation has ever produced, was saved at the age of eight. Charles Haddon Spurgeon, "the prince of preachers," was saved when he was twelve. And he later said he would have been saved earlier if there had been someone to instruct and guide him.

In my own denomination (the Southern Baptist Convention), one survey showed that 90 percent of all our missionaries were converted before they were eleven. The average age of their conversion was eight.

The early church father Polycarp was converted at nine years of age and died in the flames for Jesus at ninety. Sounds to me like that was a childhood conversion that took! Make it your joy to lead your children to Christ.

CORRECT WITH CONSISTENCY

A second child-training technique found in Proverbs 22:6 is this: you are to correct with consistency. In addition to the idea of dedication, the Hebrew word for "train" also has in it the idea of correction or discipline. We must correct our children. Let me give you some reasons for that.

Because God Says So

We have noted Proverbs 13:24—"He that spareth his rod hateth his son." Sometimes you hear a parent say, "Oh, I could never spank little Throckmorton. I just love him so much."

According to God's Word, that is a lie. A father doesn't love his child when he refuses to correct him. That father loves himself. He doesn't like the displeasure and inconvenience of having to discipline his child and then listen to him cry.

The Bible says in Hebrews 12:6 (quoting Proverbs 3:12), "Whom the Lord loveth he chasteneth." No parent is smarter than God. If you love your child, you're going to correct your child.

Because of Human Nature

Another reason you ought to correct your child with consistency is because of the nature of humanity. Consider Proverbs 22:15—"Foolishness is bound in the heart of a child; but the rod of correction shall drive it far from him."

The word "foolishness" here does not mean innocent, childish silliness. It means wickedness, in the same sense that the Bible uses the term *fool* throughout the book of Proverbs. The fool in Proverbs is someone who hates and ignores God and plunges recklessly into sin, to his own destruction.

You may say, "You mean all of that is bound up in the heart of my little angel?" Yes, in the heart of your little angel.

The behavioral psychologists told us for years that children were like little rosebuds just waiting to unfold. So you shouldn't do anything that would harm their little petals. Therefore, if Junior wants to cut the leg off the dining room table, you need to keep the saw sharp so the little darling won't be frustrated.

That's not what the Word of God says. The Bible says that children need to learn there is a moral authority in this world against which they are not allowed to rebel. And when required, we need to reinforce that lesson with the rod of correction, which we'll talk more about later. There are some things a child can learn through the seat of his pants before he's twelve that he'll only learn through great pain afterwards.

To Spare Yourself

Another reason you ought to correct your children is to save yourself a little disgrace and give yourself a little happiness. Proverbs 29:15 says, "The rod and reproof give wisdom: but a child left to himself bringeth his mother to shame." But go down to verse 17—"Correct thy son, and he shall give thee rest; yea, he shall give delight unto thy soul."

If you don't discipline your children, one of these days you're going to be ashamed for your lack of consistency. But what a joy to see children who have been well corrected.

Stop trying to win a popularity contest with your children; begin planning for their future. "Now no chastening for the present seemeth to be joyous, but grievous," the Bible says. "Nevertheless, afterward it yieldeth the peaceable fruit of righteousness unto them which are exercised thereby" (Hebrews 12:11).

A Spiritual Benefit

Here's a major reason for correcting your child with consistency: "Withhold not correction from the child: for if thou beatest him with the rod, he shall not die. Thou shalt beat him with the rod, and shalt deliver his soul from hell" (Proverbs 23:13-14).

At first glance that sounds awfully cruel. But this is not talking about child abuse. The word "rod" does not mean a club. The writer is talking about a spanking utensil, something that will cause a sting without doing any harm.

God has built every child with a spanking place. My daddy never spanked me on an empty stomach. He just turned me over! That's the spanking place God has given. And by the way, the Bible is wise to tell parents to use a spanking utensil rather than their bare hands. Use a neutral instrument for spanking so that your hands can be thought of as instruments of love and caressing.

Spanking is a form of discipline that needs to be used at the right time and at the right place in the right way. Never are you to do physical harm to a child. You can chasten a child without hurting him. And the Bible says that if you will be consistent in this, you'll save your child's soul from hell.

How is that? Well, a child who does not learn to respect authority at home is not going to respect authority in the school, the church, or the government—and will not respect God either. The great problem in America today is that we have an unruly, unwashed generation that has no respect for authority—God's or anybody else's.

This is a lesson that has to begin at home. The Bible says your child will not die from corporal punishment, even though he or she will make the neighbors think they're going to die by their howls.

The issue here is not death but life! A child who is disciplined and corrected according to the principles of God's Word will find spiritual life, not death. God's Ten Commandments are precepts that lead to life.

Seven Rules for Discipline

Here are seven basic rules for discipline learned from life and the Word of God.

The first is a repeat of what we said earlier. That is, begin your discipline early. You should begin to correct a child when that child is old enough to knowingly and willingly disobey. Some parents never get on "spanking terms" with their children. But they ought to be.

Second, think of spanking as your last resort, not the first technique you use. Resort to a spanking only when reasoning and warning and instructing have failed to bring about the desired behavior.

The Lord Jesus said, "As many as I love, I rebuke and chasten" (Revelation 3:19). First He rebukes, and then He chastens. We need to learn that we can do more with our words than we can with physical discipline. We can do more with telling and leading and teaching and explaining than we can with a paddle; so speaking ought to come before spanking.

But if you've told your child, "If you do this or that, you're going to get a spanking," keep your word. On one occasion I came down out of the pulpit when I was preaching and administered a little corporal punishment to one of my children in front of the congregation. I was an immature young man at that time, and I think now that I shouldn't have done that. But neither that child nor the congregation ever forgot it. I had told my children that if they did so and so, I was going to do such and such. Keep your word to your children if you promise them a spanking.

A third basic rule of discipline is to administer it promptly. Especially when it's time for corporal punishment, deliver the discipline as close to the time of the disobedience as possible. Don't let a threat linger over a child's head all day.

Fourth, father and mother need to present a united front in discipline. Don't let one do all the spanking and the other do all the hugging. As a matter of fact, one parent can hold the child while the other administers the discipline, and then both can hug the child when it's over. Children are very clever. They will play one parent against another if you let them. Don't fall into that trap.

Here's a fifth rule: if you decide to spank your child, do a good job. Here's what I mean. Have you ever seen a mother in a supermarket just kind of swatting at her child? The kid is dodging and feinting like a boxer as the mother flails the air. She's getting madder by the minute, and the child isn't learning anything except when to duck.

What a poor way to correct children. If you're going to administer a spanking, do it in the right place, at the right time, and in the right way. The great thing about a good spanking is that you don't have to do it very often. A few good spankings and your spanking days should be more or less over. You shouldn't have to constantly be swatting at your kids.

But if you do deliver a good and well-deserved spanking and your child is still sulking and rebellious, don't be afraid to give it another try. You can't afford to let a child leave a discipline session seething with defiant, rebellious anger. Stay with it a little bit longer.

Just in case you think I'm starting to sound like the meanest man who ever lived, let me give you a sixth rule of discipline: always discipline in love. We saw in Hebrews 12:6 that the Lord loves the ones He disciplines. Your discipline should always be an expression of your love.

The whole point of the Ten Commandments was to cause God's people to love Him with all of their being. That's what Jesus said in Matthew 22:37 when He was asked to summarize the Commandments.

The opposite of disciplining in love is provoking your children to "wrath" (Ephesians 6:4). How can you provoke a child to wrath? Well, wrath produces wrath, and nothing good can come of it. The Bible says, "The wrath of man worketh not the righteousness of God" (James 1:20).

You've heard it said before, but it's still true—never punish your child when you're angry yourself. Wrath produces wrath, bitterness produces bitterness, and love produces love. When you discipline a child in love, the message is going to come through that this disobedience has broken your heart because you love that child so much.

At the same time, don't withhold your love as a form of punishment. Chastise your children, then sit down and cry with them if that's called for, hug them, and love them.

Seventh and finally, always discipline with a view to repentance. Correction is not a matter of getting even with your child. Nor is the goal simply to administer outward correction. You want to correct the child inwardly as well as outwardly.

When your child does something that deserves a spanking, that child has sinned. The Fifth Commandment says, "Honor thy father and thy mother." Ephesians 6:1 tells children, "Obey your parents in the Lord."

When children are old enough to understand the concept of sin, they need to know that what they have done not only breaks God's law, it breaks His heart. If you as a parent can pray with a child and help that child to understand this, you have an excellent opportunity to lead the child in repenting and asking God's forgiveness.

While repentance may be your desire and your goal, you may not reach it in every case with every child. You cannot be the Holy Spirit in your child's life. You cannot make a child repent, but you can pray that he will. And you can discipline in a way that points the child in the direction of repentance toward God.

This is what it means to correct with consistency. I believe that if you will do this, God will honor it and use it in your children's lives.

COMMUNICATE WITH CREATIVITY

Let's go back to our foundational verse and notice again that Proverbs 22:6 says, "Train up a child *in the way he should go*" (my emphasis). This is a very interesting phrase that I believe tells us we should be training our children creatively.

A Child's Uniqueness

I say that because the idea behind this phrase is that every child is an individual. The word "way" actually refers to the bend in a bow. A loose translation might be something like this: "Train up a child in the way that he is naturally bent." That's really what it means.

You see, all children come into the world with a natural bent. Children are not all the same. God does not make carbon copies; He only makes originals. Your child carries within him or her a God-given blend of innate talents, interests, personality traits, and yet-to-be-developed spiritual gifts that make him or her unique—one of a kind.

Therefore, you must deal with each child as a unique individual. That means you need to be creative in your approach to each of your children. You need God's wisdom to communicate His truth with creativity because every child has a particular bent that is his and his alone.

I want to tell you, all four of the Rogers children are different. Adam and Eve had two boys, Cain and Abel, who were as different as it's possible for two brothers to be. One became a murderer, and the other became a martyr. One was wicked, and the other was a worshiper.

Isn't that amazing? Two boys coming out of the same mother's womb with the same background and the same environment—and yet they were very different. Look at the difference between Jacob and Esau, and they were even twins. Think of the sons of David—Solomon and Absalom. What a difference in the two.

Each child is unique. With some children, all you have to do is speak a word of rebuke and they melt in tears. But other kids you have to carry to the back bedroom and give them a solid spanking. There's such a difference. You need to be wise and sensitive to train up your child according to his or her bent.

One way you can accomplish this is by what you don't do. Don't try to make something out of your child that God does not want to make out of your child. Some parents try to succeed through their child and force their desires and ambitions upon him or her. But God has put a unique bent in that child's personality.

You may say, "My children aren't bent—they're warped." There is a warping that comes from sin and that needs to be straightened through nurture and discipline, as we have just talked about. But that's very different from the proclivities God has built into your child.

Teaching Creatively

In the preceding chapters we have already shared so many ways to teach the Ten Commandments and the rest of God's Word creatively. I won't try to review those here because you already have access to them.

We are often told that we can't teach Bible doctrine to little children, that they're too young to understand it. But even a little one can learn "Jesus loves me, this I know." Those little children can learn to love and reverence God. And they will live what they learn.

That's why a child who is constantly being criticized learns to condemn others. A child who lives with anger and violence learns to fight. A child who is made fun of withdraws into a shell.

But on the positive side, a child who is given encouragement gains the confidence to face life. A child who is treated with fairness develops a sense of justice. A child who is made to feel secure at home learns to trust God. A child who knows he is loved and accepted as he is accepts other people the same way. And a child who receives love gives love.

On this matter of teaching and training with creativity, let me give you a fascinating picture of what this meant in Hebrew culture. In addition to its connotations of dedication and discipline, the word *train* has in its very root the idea of touching something to the palate.

What does that mean? Hebrew mothers didn't have ready-made baby food; so the mother would strain the baby's food by chewing it up herself and then take a little bit of that food and touch it to the part of the baby's palate called the uvula.

Do you know what happens when the uvula is stimulated? It triggers the swallowing impulse. So the mother would put the food in the baby's mouth, and the baby would swallow. That's how Hebrew mothers fed their children.

What a great picture of making the Word of God palatable to our children. We can't just ram it down their throats or they'll choke on it. We must be gentle and kind. That's the problem with so many parents who try to teach the Bible to their kids. They're not teaching it creatively. The idea is, "You sit still while I instill."

That's why some kids don't like family worship. It's like cod liver oil—a dose a day keeps the devil away. That's not the way to do it. Your children are unique individuals. Find their bent, and guide them in the way God has aimed them. Then you'll find success.

CONTINUE WITH CONFIDENCE

What a wonderful picture Proverbs 22:6 gives us of the proper way to teach and train our children. If you will commence with childhood, correct with consistency, and communicate with creativity, you will continue with confidence because God's Word says, "When [your child] is old, he will not depart from it."

Now that doesn't mean when your child is a middle-aged adult or an old man. The word "old" here has the idea of hair on the chin. In other words, this is referring to a child who is able to grow a beard, which could even mean a teenager.

I must say a word about this because many brokenhearted Christian parents are clinging to Proverbs 22:6 as they wait for wayward adult children to return to the fold. The first thing we need to see is that the proverbs of Scripture are not iron-clad promises. They are principles that when applied faithfully will generally end in a desired result. But there is no guarantee because children sometimes make bad decisions of their own.

This is not to say that Proverbs 22:6 is not inspired truth. But Bible proverbs are proverbs, not promises. Remember that alongside the proverb is another factor—human will. Some parents are taking undue blame for the failures of their children, and other parents may be taking undue praise for the sheer grace of God that has given them wonderful kids.

There comes a time also when training gives way to prayer. As I said earlier, children are in our hands like arrows in the hand of a warrior, to be polished, pointed, and propelled.

When they leave our hands, we hope they will fly straight to the target. But once they are out of our hands, about all we can do (and the very best thing we can do) is pray for a good wind.

Another thing I want you to see is that this verse does not assume what so many people commonly believe about the spiritual training of children. That is, many parents have the idea that you teach your children about God when they are little, then when they're teenagers they will have a time of rebellion where they leave the right path, but as they grow up, they will eventually come back.

I've heard people say, "Well, my son is not living for God, but you know what the Bible says: 'When he is old, he'll not depart from it.'" Proverbs 22:6 doesn't promise he will come back. I know of no Bible promise that says a wayward child is certain to come back to Christ.

In the mercy of God he may return to the faith, and many older children have. But that's not what Proverbs 22:6 is talking about. It's a tremendous word of encouragement and exhortation to raise your children in the nurture and admonition of the Lord.

You say, "But my children aren't little anymore." Then start where you are. And if they're already grown, pray for them. God is so merciful!

I want you to know that you can have a successful home if you'll teach God's ancient "secrets," His Ten Commandments, to your children. You can bring your children to Christ, and you can bring them up for Christ.

Let me close with a word of personal testimony. I thank God for the abilities and the opportunities He has given me to serve Him. But I tell you honestly, it means more to me than anything to know that my children love the Lord Jesus Christ. When I take my children and grandchildren home to heaven with me, I'll say, "Thank You, Lord Jesus, it was worth it all."

Will you be able to say that? I trust you will.

May God bless you and help you to make your home a little touch of heaven on earth!

NOTES

Chapter 1: It Takes God to Make a Home

1. Jonathan Alter and Pat Wingert, "The Return of Shame," *Newsweek*, February 6, 1995, p. 21.
2. Kenneth L. Woodward, "What Ever Happened to Sin?" *Newsweek*, February 6, 1995, p. 23.
3. David Blankenhorn, *Fatherless America* (New York: Basic Books, 1995), p. 1.

Chapter 2: One God Per Family

1. Os Guinness and John Seel, eds., *No God but God* (Chicago: Moody Press, 1992), p. 28.
2. Josh McDowell and Bob Hostetler, *Right from Wrong* (Dallas: Word, 1994), pp. 15-16.
3. Hugh Ross, *The Creator and the Cosmos* (Chicago: Moody Press, 1993), pp. 10-11.
4. Ibid., p. 11.

Chapter 4: The Name Above All Names

1. William Hendriksen, *New Testament Commentary: Philippians* (Grand Rapids, Mich.: Baker, 1977), p. 118.
2. Jerry B. Jenkins, "A Powerful Memory," *Moody Magazine*, November 1994, p. 6.

Chapter 6: Has the Nuclear Family Bombed?

1. Raymond I. Lindquist, *Notes for Living* (New York: J. B. Lippincott Company, 1968), p. 35.
2. Dan Quayle, "Prepared Remarks by the Vice-President at the Commonwealth Club," *San Francisco*, May 19, 1992, p. 6; quoted in Robert Lewis with Rich Campbell, *Real Family Values* (Gresham, Oreg.: Vision House, 1994), p. 48.
3. Charles Swindoll, *Father: Masculine Model of Leadership* (Portland: Multnomah, 1990), p. 11; quoted in Lewis and Campbell, *Real Family Values*, p. 172.
4. Ted Koppel, "The Vannatizing of America," *Duke Magazine*, July/August 1987, p. 36.

Chapter 7: Families That Choose Life

1. R. Kent Hughes, *Disciplines of Grace* (Wheaton, Ill.: Crossway Books, 1993), p. 111.

2. George Wald, *The Collapse of Evolution*; quoted in *Evolution: Fact, Fraud, or Faith?* (Largo, Fla.: Freedom Publications, 1994), p. 236.
3. Ibid.
4. Landrun Shettles and David Rorvik, *Rites of Life: The Scientific Evidence of Life Before Birth* (Grand Rapids, Mich.: Zondervan, 1983), p. 103; quoted in Lewis and Campbell, *Real Family Values*, p. 272.

Chapter 8: The Key to a Magnificent Marriage

1. Hughes, *Disciplines of Grace*, p. 130.

Chapter 9: Honesty: Don't Leave Home Without It

1. Donald Wildmon, *Think on These Things* (Tupelo, Miss.: Five Star Publications, 1973), p. 20.
2. Chuck Colson and Jack Eckerd, *Why America Doesn't Work* (Dallas: Word, 1991), p. 58.
3. Ibid.
4. Ibid., pp. 76-77.
5. Ibid., pp. 80-81.
6. Ibid., p. 117.

Chapter 10: Truth or Consequences

1. Hughes, *Disciplines of Grace*, p. 155.
2. Clifton Fadiman, gen. ed., *The Little, Brown Book of Anecdotes* (Boston: Little, Brown, and Company, 1985), p. 555.

Chapter 11: The Secret of Satisfaction

1. Fadiman, gen. ed., *The Little, Brown Book of Anecdotes*, p. 416.

Dr. Adrian Rogers, founder and president of Love Worth Finding Ministries, is heard over syndicated radio, television, and cable systems throughout North America and many parts of the world. For broadcast and other information, call 1-800-274-5683 or write:

Love Worth Finding Ministries
Box 38-300
Memphis, Tennessee 38183.